Nurturing the Whole Child

Montessori Principles Applied to the Catechesis of Children

Gianna Gobbi

Foreword by Sofia Cavalletti
Translated and edited by Rebekah Rojcewicz

Catechesis of
the Good Shepherd
Publications

Nihil Obstat
Deacon David Keene, PHD
Chancellor
Archdiocese of Chicago
January 18, 2024

Imprimatur
Most Rev. Robert G. Casey
Vicar General
Archdiocese of Chicago
January 18, 2024

Catechesis of the Good Shepherd Publications is an imprint of Liturgy Training Publications (LTP). Further information about these publications is available from LTP or from The United States Association of The Catechesis of the Good Shepherd, 7655-A East Main Street, Scottsdale, AZ 85251; 480-874-3759; email: cgs@cgsusa.org. Requests for all other aspects of the Catechesis should be directed to this address.

Michael A. Dodd was the production editor, Juan Alberto Castillo was the designer, and Kari Nicholls was the production artist.

English translation from Italian by Rebekah Rojcewicz.

28 27 26 25 24 1 2 3 4 5

Printed in the United States of America

Library of Congress Control Number: 2023949238

ISBN: 978-1-61671-780-3

NWC

Contents

Translator/Editor's Note

Gianna Gobbi (*right*) and Rebekah Rojcewicz share a moment while on a tour of Sapienza University in the early 1980s.

It is with great joy that, through our imprint with Liturgy Training Publications, we are able to publish this new edition of Gianna Gobbi's precious contribution to the Catechesis of the Good Shepherd (CGS). Gianna's work is instrumental to our understanding of the Montessori principles that are foundational to CGS.

Gianna was Sofia Cavalletti's closest collaborator in developing the Catechesis over almost fifty years. A devoted Montessori practitioner before meeting Sofia, she brought all her wisdom, experience, and passion for the child as teacher to the search for how "the mystery of the child meets the mystery of God," as our catechesis has been referred to.

This text was originally a collection of Gianna's reflections and talks that were bound together (referred to in Italian as *la dispenza di Gianna*) to be shared with catechist formation course participants. In 1996, I was given the task of translating this text for publication in English. As I did so, I also offered edits to reflect some of the more recent discoveries Sofia and Gianna had made. Foremost among these was their important discovery that the child's relationship with the Good Shepherd is on a much higher plane than that of the child's finding in the Good Shepherd a kind of maternal safety and protection. Rather, after many years of observation of young children, Sofia and Gianna had realized that the young child finds in the Good Shepherd a true match to his or her own abundant capacity for love, wonder, and delight. The children's relationship with Jesus, the Good Shepherd, flourishes on the higher plane of friendship. Sofia and Gianna read and approved all my edits, and the text was eventually published as *Listening to God with Children: The Montessori Method Applied to the Catechesis of Children,* in 1998.

This new version of that original text includes editorial corrections and Gianna's additional insights after the book's publication. Others contribute reflections on the impact of Gianna's person and work (see appendix). The enriched content of this new publication merits a new title, and one that was originally considered when Gianna's book was first published: *Nurturing the Whole Child: Montessori Principles Applied to the Catechesis of Children*. This edition orients us to the foundational Montessori principles that are inseparable from our work in CGS and helps us to know better the heart and genius of our beloved cofounder. Yet, like all other CGS core texts, it cannot replace a formation course experience if we are to nurture the whole child in the atrium.

—Rebekah Rojcewicz

FOREWORD

In the following pages, Gianna Gobbi presents in a simple, clear, and essential way certain educational principles of the Montessori vision. But this is not just a book on theory, because we find in it the fundamentals of Montessori's thought, which Gobbi has experienced extensively and first-hand with children of different social backgrounds, of different countries, and of different intellectual abilities. Here, Montessori's educational theory, which Gobbi has assimilated through listening to Montessori speak, as well as through her attentive and extensive studies of Montessori's written work, is enlivened by Gobbi's own work "in the field." Thus, this book is a rich and living work.

Gobbi's theoretical preparation is in no way inferior to her understanding of the child. Indeed, we find in these pages the expression of a knowledge acquired through study, which converges and is in balance with a knowledge acquired through direct contact with the child, and this forms a whole. We point especially to the last chapter on prayer, where the author presents the various levels of intensity in prayer and suggests how we might assist the child's prayer. All her advice, even the smallest detail, is permeated by the living relationship Gobbi has with Montessori's thought and with the child.

As the subtitle of this book indicates, the Montessori principles being delineated herein are primarily oriented toward the religious life of the child, the manifestations of which Gobbi has studied in a particular way. Above all, it is the child who shines forth from these pages and the essential structure of the child's person, in which the relationship with the transcendent is of primary importance.

In the course of her initial experience with religious education, Montessori observed that religious education appeared to be a point of arrival, a sort of culmination of all the child does in the school, conferring new meaning on all of the child's other activities. Moreover, as Montessori noted, as a result of the atrium experience, the child exhibited a "a sense of gratitude, joy and new dignity."[1] This means that the capacities of the child are not fully realized unless the child finds his or her voice in relation to the transcendent, albeit by pathways that might differ.

Therefore, the field of experience that Gobbi deals with in these pages is not a partial and secondary area in the child's formation. Furthermore, it is not a subject that is limited to believers of a particular profession of faith. Rather, it will be of interest to anyone who seriously approaches the child and considers the child in all his or her spiritual potential.

Montessori principles are certainly a continuous thread in this book; yet Gobbi's discussion of these principles is not intended to replace one's direct reading of Maria Montessori's work to which the author refers, frequently giving precise quotations. Gobbi's purpose is to offer a preview to Montessori's thought so as to invite the reader to seek an in-depth knowledge that can only be reached by reading Maria Montessori's books and by living her ideas in direct contact with the child.

—Sofia Cavalletti

1. Maria Montessori, *The Discovery of the Child*, The Montessori Series, vol. 1 (Amsterdam: Montessori-Pierson Publishing, reprinted 2019), 316.

Preface

In her book *The Absorbent Mind*, Maria Montessori offers teachers a prayer, which she refers to as "an invitation, a kind of syllabus:" "Help us, O God, to enter into the secret of childhood, so that we may know, love and serve the child in accordance with the laws of thy justice and following thy holy will."

"To enter into the secret of childhood" requires of us, as adults, both a willing spirit and a particular discipline. Above all, this discipline comes as a result of patient observation of the children in addition to a careful preparation of ourselves, so that we can understand what we observe and know best how to respond to the child's self-revelation. Thus, those who desire "to enter into the secret of childhood" will understand the importance of further reading and formal courses in the Montessori method and in the Catechesis of the Good Shepherd, as well as guided observations of children, both in Montessori Children's Houses and in atriums.

No book can serve as a substitute for catechists' formation courses along with observation of and experience with children. Our aim in this book is simply to *mettere a fuoco* (set afire) the Montessori principles that have guided us in our ongoing quest to "know, love, and serve the child," especially in regard to his or her relationship with God. It is our hope that these pages might also serve as invitation and inspiration to all who seek "to enter the secret of childhood" and to journey with the child toward God.

Gianna Gobbi

Chapter 1

The Environment

The Importance and Function of the Environment

The word *environment* is rich in meaning. It can refer to all that surrounds the living organisms of the earth or universe. It can also mean the atmosphere or conditions of a particular location. The unique features of specific biological environments are crucial for the development and survival of various forms of life. A fish, for example, cannot live out of water.

Human beings have the capacity to adapt themselves to almost any biological environment. However, human beings also need another kind of environment, one in which the cultural, social, and moral characteristics of their time and place are manifested. The family is the first and most important environment experienced by human beings. As humans mature, we come under the influence of the environments of various religious, social, educational, and government institutions. For example, the environment for our religious life is the community of believers, the Church. Therefore, we can say that human environments differ not only in their physical and climatic conditions, but also in their purpose and significance. What the person needs, wants, or seeks to achieve in any particular environment will differ. Accordingly, the person's activity or work will differ in each environment.

Modern pedagogy often emphasizes the importance of the environment in the formation of the human being. Yet, already in the early 1900s, Maria Montessori devoted herself to the preparation of the learning environment that would foster independence and self-control in the child. She also devoted herself to the observation of children within this prepared environment, and there she made profound discoveries about the child. When, on January 6, 1907, in a poor section of Rome, Maria Montessori opened the first *Casa de Bambini* Children's House (the term she used instead of *school*), an experience of scientific pedagogy was initiated that has spread throughout the world. Over the years, this method revealed and continues to reveal Montessori's ingenious discovery of the child. Moreover, the Montessori method is a revelation of the child's interests and needs.[1]

Montessori observed two particular characteristics in the child's development that serve as guiding principles in the preparation of the environment:

- An absorbent mind (capable of assimilating information from the surrounding environment naturally—that is, without conscious effort); and
- Sensitive periods (when the child is in a particularly receptive stage of development, characterized by high interest, pertaining to various physical, intellectual, or spiritual areas).

The child's environment can assist or hinder these two characteristics. Therefore, it is important to prepare the environment so that it corresponds to the child's needs and fosters the full development of his or her personality. The environment consists of persons and things that are placed there, both of which serve as indirect tools of education. It is the task of the adult to prepare these tools in accordance with the age and changing needs of the child. The things we prepare for the child are the expression of the adult who knows how to observe the child, so that we can say the environment is constructed under the guidance of that which the child has indicated as being suitable to himself.

Within this prepared environment Montessori observed previously unrecognized characteristics of the child's behavior:

- constancy of work
- obedience
- order
- intellectual progress
- capacity for silence

1. For an in-depth study of Montessori's concept of the environment, it is suggested that one read Maria Montessori, *The Discovery of the Child*, The Montessori Series, vol. 1 (Amsterdam: Montessori-Pierson Publishing, reprinted 2019).

- concentration
- spontaneous absorption of culture

Thus, the environment needs to become a scientifically prepared environment, which is, itself, both educator and builder. The environment is essential to the construction of the human person and is, therefore, of crucial importance in educating the child to independence and stimulating the child's industry and self-control.

The Environment for Religious Education: The Atrium

Like all forms of life, religious life needs a prepared environment in order to develop and flourish. We want to prepare an environment that corresponds to the vital religious needs of the child, a place where the child can experience religious life and can come to know the realities that feed this life.

Maria Montessori envisioned a place within the school (the Children's House) that would be dedicated to the child's religious education.[2] She called this place the *atrium*, corresponding to the name of the space in the ancient basilica that lay between the street and the inner sanctum of the church. This space was an entryway or foyer, and it was in this place (often a covered courtyard) that the faithful prepared themselves, both physically and spiritually, to enter the church and to participate in the liturgy.

Montessori understood that the atrium environment, like the Children's House or any other educational environment, must foster independence, mastery of self and the environment, and the opportunity and ability to choose appropriate activity. Montessori referred to this freely chosen activity as the child's "work" and viewed it as an expression of a vital need within the child.

However, the atrium environment has its own particular characteristics and purpose. It differs from the Children's House or classroom in its atmosphere of solemnity. The atrium serves as an intermediary between the classroom and the Church, and like the environment of the church, it is a place where the child can listen to the proclamation

2. Maria Montessori, *The Child in the Church*, ed. E. M. Standing (St. Paul, MN: Catechetical Guild, 2017), chap. 11.

of the Good News, meditate on it, and begin to live it according to the child's own rhythm. Different from the environment of the church, the atrium is not only a place for announcement and celebration, it is also a place for work. It is a particular environment in which work easily becomes meditation and prayer.

The original Level 1 atrium in Rome

The atrium environment requires an interior design and arrangement of furniture and materials that will facilitate the child's work. In a way, it will resemble an adult retreat center, which is also prepared so that the external elements aid concentration and meditation. In an adult retreat center, the adult might find help for his or her meditation and prayer in books—whereas, in the atrium, the child finds this help in the catechetical materials.

The interior design of the atrium must correspond to the child's developmental needs and must allow for freedom of movement. The furniture will be child-sized, and the materials will be accessible and easily handled by the child. The whole environment must serve as a guide and lead the way to the order and organization of the work that ought to develop in this space.

The Prayer Corner

The arrangement of furnishings and materials in the space will serve as a reminder of and a guide to the subjects to be presented during the course of the year. In the atrium of the younger children (ages 3–6) the material of the parable of the Good Shepherd will occupy a central space. Special care will be given to the preparation of the prayer corner, which will include an honored place for the Holy Bible. (See chapter 15 on prayer for a detailed description of the prayer corner.)

There will be an area in the atrium dedicated to baptism and another dedicated to the small model of the altar, with miniature sacred vessels stored in a sacristy cabinet. Dioramas of the infancy narratives are flanked by a raised-surface map of the Land of Israel. Other materials address parables of the kingdom, the Last Supper, gestures of the Mass, and so on.

The Baptism Corner

These materials are presented one by one to the children in an order and in a manner that invites the children to work with them and lends a certain order and clarity to their work. Once established, the order with which things are presented and used is respected by the adult, who shows the children the proper place and use of these things.

At the beginning of the atrium sessions, along with the proclamation and meditation on the Word or the liturgy, the catechist will demonstrate the use of materials in the atrium. It is important for the child's mastery of the environment and ability to choose appropriate work that materials be added gradually to the atrium and not all set out at the beginning of the atrium year.

Furthermore, the external order of the environment—how and where things are placed, as well as their consistent placement week after week—is important for the child's sense of security and empowers the child to utilize the environment more fully. Montessori said that, indeed, the child should enter the Children's House (or, in our case, the atrium) and be able to picture the space in his or her mind. The child may then experience the delight of knowing every object and where to find each one.

The Religious Environment in the Family

The development of the child's religious life begins in the family environment from the very beginning of the child's life. The following are simple suggestions for nurturing the child's religious life within the family and the Church, which offer the child a way of participating in the family's faith life and of expressing the child's own religious characteristics and needs:

- When the child is nursing or lying down, parents can place near the child an image of the Risen Christ on the cross or of the infant Jesus in his Mother's arms. Parents should simply point out and name the image for the child.
- Ritual gestures, such as making the sign of the cross or blessing the food, are very important for the child to see. Parents can do the gestures slowly and deliberately, either in silence or accompanied by words of prayer.
- Parents can bless their child after giving physical care, especially after administering medicine or a bandage.
- Parents and family members can pray next to the child in bed or sing hymns in a soft voice while the baby is nursing.
- Parents can prepare a prayer space for the child in his or her bedroom or in another place in the home. This space may resemble the prayer corner in the atrium (see chapter 15 on prayer). In the evening, the whole family might gather at this space for a simple prayer time. The child will love the daily repetition of such a ritual.
- Parents should begin to take the child to church with them at a very early age, allowing the child to take in the environment: the people, the actions of the priest, the sounds, and the smells. It is helpful to sit near enough to the altar so that the child can see the actions and feel part of it. Parents can simply name things or moments in the liturgy. It is also helpful with very young children to enter after the Liturgy of the Word, as this part of the Mass is not easily understood by them and can make the Mass too long for them.

The following points reiterate what has alread been covered in this chapter:

- The atrium is a place for the proclamation of and response to the Word of God.
- We can say that the atrium is "Mass-centered." This means that the work of the atrium focuses on the relationship with Jesus, the Good Shepherd, which "finds its most concrete and intense moment of life in the Eucharist."[3] (Accordingly, the material called "The Eucharistic Presence of the Good Shepherd" sits

3. Sofia Cavalletti, *The Religious Potential of the Child* (Chicago: Catechesis of the Good Shepherd Publications, 2020), 25.

alongside the parable of the Good Shepherd material in the center of the room.)

- In the atrium the child handles materials and experiences ritual celebrations like those seen and experienced in church. This includes
    - the changing of colors according to the liturgical time;
    - prayers according to the liturgical time;
    - liturgical rites celebrated with solemnity and in a form suitable to the child's pace and capabilities. (For example, when we celebrate the solemn Easter Vigil in the atrium, we choose only certain key moments and prayers of the Liturgy of the Light so that the children may experience them more fully.)
- The experiences the child has in the atrium serve as an invitation to and preparation for the liturgical life they will share with adults in the church.
- In the atrium the child is free to choose his or her own work, according to his or her ability to do so.
    - The atrium is an environment that is carefully prepared to foster the religious life of the child. The materials and images placed there help the child to concentrate and reflect; thus, they nurture the child's natural capacity for contemplation.

In order to set up an atrium, time and care are needed but not excessive amounts of money. Atriums are sometimes created in unusual places and with chance furnishings. In the parish of Santa Maria in Aquiro, Italy, the pastor cleaned and reorganized the storage areas of the church to be an atrium, using castoff items to furnish it. A nun restored and adapted her convent's stable to an atrium. In a poor quarter of Mexico, a community made their own bricks and built an atrium. Atriums have been established in choir lofts and even in garages. Often, atriums have begun in homes until space could be made available in the church. The atrium will reflect the conditions and characteristics of the place, the culture, the economic and social capacities of the group that organizes it.

Chapter 2

The Role of the Adult

As noted, it is the adult's task to carefully prepare the environment for the child. Yet the most carefully prepared environment will be of little use if the catechist, himself or herself, is not also carefully prepared. In this vein, Maria Montessori said that the things we prepare must be the external expression of a most profound transformation that carries us to a particular attitude of "educator" (or, in our case: educator-catechist).

The environment and materials are meant to be indirect instruments of education. They speak to the child without words and invite the child's personal and freely chosen activity. Furthermore, the environment and materials are very important for the adult, because they help him or her to refrain from unnecessary interventions in the child's work. More importantly, they allow the adult to get out of the way so that the true Teacher, the Holy Spirit, can operate fully.

However, the atrium environment and materials alone would be insufficient. Christianity is a religion that requires a proclamation, an announcement of the Good News. Besides preparing the environment, the task of the catechist is to proclaim the Good News. Moreover, it is the catechist who, in effect, brings the environment and materials to life. He or she entices and guides the children in their use of the environment. The catechist does this with great care and respect in order to safeguard the child's autonomy and authentic, personal response.

In her book *The Discovery of the Child*, Maria Montessori wrote beautifully about the preparation of the teacher, wherein she reflects on the attitude that the teacher needs to have in order to work with the child.[1] These pages can also serve as a guide in the formation of the catechist.

Montessori lifts up as a model the figure of the scientist, who, with passionate attention and loss of self-awareness, observes and investigates nature. This spirit of patience and persistence is what qualifies the scientist, not the instruments or methods used. Scientists exercise great patience in repeating the experiment again and again, waiting for the results that might come. As they gradually discover things that are always more profound and wondrous, scientists also exercise humility in becoming aware of their own smallness before the grandeur of nature and in realizing that these wonders do not belong to them.

Clearly then, there is an attitude that distinguishes the scientist and goes beyond the mechanics or technique involved. We might say that the scientist is fully a scientist only when the spirit supersedes the technique. According to Montessori, in addition to knowledge of educative instruments and methods, the teacher must have the spirit of the scientist, and this spirit needs preparation and nurturance. She writes in *The Discovery of the Child*: "I consider that we ought to infuse in teachers the spirit rather than the mechanism of the scientist; that is, the aim of training ought to be directed toward the spirit rather than toward the machinery."[2] What counts, then, is knowing how to be a humble and patient observer.

In her book *Spontaneous Activity in Education*, Montessori says that "one who is impatient cannot appraise things properly; he can only appreciate his own impulses and his own satisfactions."[3] In order to overcome this state of impatience, a real education is required. This attitude is essential if teachers are to accomplish their complex and challenging duties.

Montessori goes on to spell out the characteristics of what she calls "the new teacher." She writes: "Instead of facility in speech, she has to acquire the power of silence; instead of teaching, she has to

1. Maria Montessori, *The Discovery of the Child*, The Montessori Series, vol. 1 (Amsterdam: Montessori-Pierson Publishing, reprinted 2019), chap. 1.
2. Montessori, *The Discovery of the Child*, 5.
3. Maria Montessori, *The Advanced Montessori Method, Volume I: Scientific Pedagogy as Applied to the Education of Children*, The Montessori Series, vol. 9 (Amsterdam: Montessori-Pierson Publishing, reprinted 2018), 100.

observe; instead of the proud dignity of one who claims to be infallible, she assumes the vesture of humility."[4]

If this attitude of patience and humility is right and necessary in every field of education, it is even more important in religious education, where nothing belongs to the adult, neither the soul of the child nor what is being offered to the child. All that is being transmitted belongs to God and is given by God out of God's goodness and for our joy. The child, as a living being, is a being in development. The adult educator is given the privilege of assisting and consciously participating in a creative act, but he or she must not forget that only a part in it is reserved for him or her, and not even the principal part.[5]

A. M. Joosten concluded the Twenty-Third Indian Montessori Course for teachers in New Delhi, March 9, 1959, by saying: "We must not give a form to the child, and we must not even try to do so, because it would not be the child's own form. We must help the child to manifest the form for which he was created, and it must not be for us to decide. The child must be helped to reveal the form which truly belongs to him and to the Creator, who is Creator of all things that are, that were, and that will be, and who loves all that He brings forth."

The first step in solving the problem of education should be directed not to children but to educators. Teachers must be willing to relinquish preconceived ideas and prejudices about the child. "Another step follows this one: we must prepare an environment adapted to the child's life, one that is free of obstacles. . . . The adult must give and do what is necessary for the child to act for himself; if the adult does less than is necessary, the child cannot act meaningfully, and if the adult does more than is necessary, he imposes himself upon the child, extinguishing the child's creative impulses. . . . The teacher remains in her capacity as director and guide, but only when necessary; the child's personality arises according to its own laws, exercising its abilities to act."[6]

---

4. Montessori, *The Advanced Montessori Method, Volume I*, 97.
5. Sofia Cavalletti, *The Religious Potential of the Child* (Chicago: Catechesis of the Good Shepherd Publications, 2020), chap. 12.
6. Maria Montessori, *The Child in the Family*, The Montessori Series, vol. 8 (Amsterdam: Montessori-Pierson Publishing, reprinted 2007), 67, 68.

Therefore, the adult must take on the work of self-transformation. Montessori suggested, in fact, that the adult's work with the child be preceded by an examination of conscience, acknowledging the two capital sins of pride and anger. The pride arises from overvaluing our part in forming the child; the anger is kindled when the child, whom we consider in some way to be our possession, doesn't respond as we expected.

The educator-catechist must be very clear on two points that are basic to one's relationship with the child in the learning environment: (1) one's role as helper and guide; and (2) the importance of the child's personal work.

The educator-catechist directs the activity of the child in a discreet manner, leaving the child to continue on his or her own whenever the child is capable of doing so. Unfortunately, we often make the mistake of misjudging the child's capabilities and intervening at the wrong time, and, in so doing, we interfere with the child's normal path of development. Instead, we must be ready to intervene when the child truly needs our help. Moreover, we must sharpen our ability to recognize this need, even when the child does not express it in words.

Regarding religious education, the first moment necessarily involves proclaiming the Word. Then the catechist must know how to step aside and allow the Word itself to do its work in the child. It is the Holy Spirit, present in God's Word, who engages the child in a personal dialogue and is, thus, the true Teacher.

In her book *The Religious Potential of the Child*, Sofia Cavalletti writes, "The adult who is to proclaim the most essential points of the Christian message, to listen to it with the children, and to observe the children in order to know their needs, must remind himself that he is the 'unworthy servant' of the Gospel."[7]

Catechesis should be a religious experience that is shared by adults and children. Children and adults listen to God's Word together. Since the adult serves as a sort of mediator, his or her attitude must be one, not only of faith, but also of profound humility and sincerity. The catechist needs to have a clear awareness of his or her own boundaries regarding the intimate relationship between the child and God, and

7. Cavalletti, *The Religious Potential of the Child*, 23.

these boundaries must not be crossed. In proclaiming the Word of God, the catechist needs a method that allows the child to come into direct contact with that Word. But, above all, the catechist needs an attitude of humility and respect.

Chapter 3

The Role of the Material

The materials placed in the prepared environment are not, first of all, teacher's aids—that is, aids to the teacher's lessons or presentations. The material is designed for the personal work of the children.

In the Montessori Children's House the sensorial materials are intended to develop and refine the children's senses. These materials are objects grouped according to specific physical properties, such as color, form, dimension, tactile qualities, sound, weight, temperature, and so on. They attract and interest the child and engage him or her in a freely chosen activity.

In the same way the alphabet enables us to read, the sensorial materials serve as a guide to the overall environment, bringing order and clarity to impressions the child absorbs there. Thus, the sensorial materials are also a guide to the spontaneous work of the child, leading to repetition of the exercise and to concentration. For older children in the elementary school we also make use of material that tends toward abstraction and that assists the child in the development of his or her personality and the acquisition of culture.

Material of the Catechesis of the Good Shepherd

The materials used in the Catechesis of the Good Shepherd are not meant to lead to the formulation of concepts, but to a vital encounter with a real Person. Therefore, we can say that the child's use of the materials leads not to the consideration of ideas, but to prayer. They are not only an aid to learning, but they are also an aid to religious life itself. The catechetical materials concretize the religious realities, both from the Bible and the liturgy, which are being proclaimed or lifted up in the atrium. The materials help make these realities tangible and visible for the child and help the child to absorb them.

As we have said, the material, as well as the whole prepared environment, is also a help to the adults present. It allows them to assume their servant role with discretion and respect, while ensuring the autonomy of the child and stimulating his or her personal work.

The catechist first makes the proclamation during a brief presentation to the children, which includes a demonstration of the proper use of the relevant material. After the catechist has shown the children how to put the material back in its proper place, the children are invited to make individual choices of the materials in the atrium to which they have been previously introduced and with which they want to work. For the most part, the child will work with his or her chosen material without the direct assistance of the adult. Thus, the material can offer an opportunity for an interior dialogue between the child and the true Teacher.

Within the prepared environment the children are free to choose their own work. Moreover, they demonstrate the capacity to choose materials that correspond to the particular developmental phase they are passing through. The child may repeat the exercise as many times as desired and often does so with great concentration and with intense silence, thereby achieving a sort of spontaneous self-discipline. It is in such moments as these that the child internalizes what has been proclaimed and makes it his or her own.

For example, the catechist presents the parable of the Good Shepherd in this way:

- The catechist briefly introduces the parable to orient the children to listen to the theme and invite them to listen to the biblical text.
- The catechist lights a candle and solemnly reads the text from the Bible.
- The catechist introduces the material and makes very simple movements with the figures in accordance with the text as it is read again.
- The catechist invites the reflections and prayerful responses of the children to the text. (This is done with the utmost care and respect. The catechist never forces a particular response. Indeed, the catechist recognizes that silence is often the deepest response that could be offered.)

- The catechist then shows the children how and where the material is put away.
- The catechist invites the children to work. Very often the children, even the most restless ones, will separate themselves from their peers in order to focus on their chosen work. They exhibit unusual peacefulness and joy and often go on working for a long time. At other times they come out with spontaneous comments or proclamations, making connections between their own life and something experienced in the atrium. For example, the Good Shepherd might suddenly remind them of someone dear to them, someone with whom they've experienced particular love and care, such as their mother, father, sibling, or friend.

In addition to helping put the child in touch with great religious realities, the materials also invite and encourage controlled movement. Early in the atrium year the focus of the presentations is on nomenclature and movement. Through what Montessori called "lessons of practical life" the children are introduced to the things in their environment and are shown how to do simple tasks involving the care of self and the environment. They are shown simple movements, like how to move around the atrium, how to sit, how to carry things, how to put things away, and so on.

The catechist also demonstrates the simple how-tos of social interaction or, what Montessori called, "lessons of grace and courtesy." The early presentations of the model altar involve naming the articles of the Mass and inviting the child to an experience of controlled movement in setting up the model altar for himself or herself.

Learning to master one's own body is an important step for the young child in gaining confidence as well as the ability to concentrate. Both of these capacities are tied to the capacity for prayer, which involves being peaceful or at rest within oneself in order to focus on and listen to God. Religious experience is a deep need of the child and must involve his or her whole person. It is important that young children receive religious content not only through presentations of the Word and the liturgy, but also through the movements and gestures that they carry out themselves.

For the most part, there will only be one of each thing in the atrium: one Good Shepherd set, one annunciation diorama, and so on. One of each thing in the atrium is meant to help the children experience real community life. They more readily learn to wait and to consider alternate options, as well as to share. However, it is also important that the young child not be rushed or pressured to stop his or her work so another child can have a turn. From the beginning of the year, the simple rule is established that until a child has finished with the material and has returned it to its place, others may not take it. Instead, they must wait, either by watching nearby or choosing another activity.

Therefore, care must also be given to ensure that there are enough materials and activities for all the children in the atrium at any given moment. These criteria are easily met if one considers the variety of activities available in the area of practical life (such as flower arranging, folding, polishing), art (such as drawing or painting), and handwork (such as pasting, tracing).

Characteristics of the Catechetical Material

Everything in the educational environment, in this case the atrium, affects the child's physical, psychological, intellectual, and spiritual formation. All the persons, the room arrangement, the furnishings, and the materials play a part, either directly or indirectly, in helping (or hindering) the child in the development of self-control, concentration, reasoning, and reflection.

The materials prepared for the children's use in the atrium are meant to facilitate meditation and lead to prayer. After a presentation from the Word or the liturgy, the catechist demonstrates the use of a relevant material and invites the children to work with it. The child's work with the material engages more than the child's senses or mind; it helps put him or her in touch with the true Teacher, the Holy Spirit, who speaks to the child of spiritual truths, of hidden, transcendent realities and calls the child into deeper relationship with God.

Liturgical signs concretize transcendent reality. For example, the water of baptism is the sign of God's gift to us of new life, the life of the Risen Christ. Christ himself is present in the Eucharist under the appearances of bread and wine. One of our tasks as catechists is to help the child learn to read the signs—that is, to help them perceive and grasp the transcendent realities hidden in the concrete and material sign. The catechetical materials are designed in accordance with the "method of signs" as found in the liturgy and about which Sofia Cavalletti speaks at length in *The Religious Potential of the Child.*[1]

A particular Montessori principle that is applied to the catechetical material is that of "isolation of difficulty." This means that each material focuses on or isolates a particular theological point (not many at the same time). For example, the first presentation of baptism focuses only on the signs of the paschal light and the white garment; the presentation of Epiclesis isolates the downward gesture with open hands, which the priest does to invoke the Holy Spirit, and so on.

Any material that accompanies the Christian Proclamation (whether the proclamation is from Scripture or liturgy) must be very specific; it must be strictly linked to the content of the proclamation. Just as the catechist's presentation must be very simple and essential, focusing on a very few theological aspects or doctrinal points, so also the material must be simple, essential, and limited in the formal elements of the doctrinal content which it is made to stress. For example, each infancy narrative (the Annunciation, Visitation, Nativity, and so on) has its own diorama and figures.

Diorama of the annunciation

Like the oral presentation, the material lifts up the essential religious content without superfluous additions or embellishments. We say, then, that the material must be objective. Furthermore, it must be made in such a way that it can speak directly to the child.

An authentic material does not spring from the imagination of the adult. It is not the product of the adult's inventiveness or creativity, even though such a material might be stimulating or interesting to the adult. Rather, a true material must speak to the child; it must call the child to a work, to an activity that touches his or her vital need.

1. Sofia Cavalletti, *The Religious Potential of the Child: Experiencing Scripture and Liturgy with Young Children*, 3rd ed. (Chicago: Catechesis of the Good Shepherd Publications, 2020), 125–134.

In the child's personal work with the material there is the experience of discovery and conquest, of taking a step forward in the formation of his or her person.

Glass cruets

The catechist must select materials with careful attention to the details of color, texture, and harmony of shapes that will attract and interest the child. Every aspect of the material can be significant in facilitating the child's work and encouraging repetition and concentration. For example, any vessel for pouring should be proportioned to the child's hands and not too heavy. Little cruets must have mouths shaped that enable the child to pour the liquid slowly and smoothly.

The meticulous care given to preparing or choosing the right material might seem excessive, but the details help the child focus on the doctrinal content of the presentation. For example, the materials used for the presentation of the Epiclesis are a medium-sized glass chalice, a small glass plate, and a paper model of the host. The direct aim of the presentation is to isolate the liturgical sign of the gesture.

Material for the epiclesis

The catechist slowly, silently makes a downward gesture with open hands over the model chalice and paten and then invites the children to read the sign: Where does the gesture begin? Where does it go? What could it mean? Through the gesture itself, the child can begin to "see" the descent of the Holy Spirit on the altar.

This presentation also paves the way for later presentations that continue to nurture the child's deep capacity for understanding God's greatest gift: Jesus, the Good Shepherd, made present to us in the bread and wine, through the power of the Holy Spirit.

For this particular presentation on the gesture of epiclesis it is not necessary to have anything in the chalice. The children already know that there would be wine in the chalice at Mass. (We use actual wine in the atrium for other presentations on the Mass.) Because young children are in a sensitive period for movement, the pouring of wine into the chalice would distract them from the primary movement of this presentation: the gesture of epiclesis.

The presence of the paper host, on the other hand, is not a distraction; it is simply a concrete reminder of the Eucharistic moment from which this gesture is taken. What is of utmost importance here is that we help the children see and learn to read the gestures of the Mass. These gestures speak to us; they speak to us of who God is and of our relationship with God.

After isolation of difficulty, the second most important Montessori principle is control of error. Both the overall environment and the specific materials must offer the possibility for the child to see his or her own mistakes and attend to self-correction. For example, actual glass objects, not plastic, are used because if these objects are not handled carefully, they will break.[2] Light-colored furniture enables the child to see spills and stains that he or she needs to clean up. In this way, the "control of error" factor fosters attentiveness, reasoning, and responsible action; thus, it also serves indirectly in moral formation.

In the catechetical materials themselves, unlike the Montessori sensorial or didactic materials, there are actually very few instances of control of error. Rather, the catechetical materials are simply faithful to the doctrinal content being proclaimed. Indeed, neither their message nor the resonance of their message within the child are subject to control.

Finally, it is important that, as much as possible, the catechist make his or her own catechetical material. Making the materials by hand is an essential way of entering more deeply into the theme we will present to the children. It helps us to slow down and to pace ourselves

2. The children learn very quickly to control their movements and not break things. Using these controlled movements is beneficial to brain development. Should something break, the children are shown how to carefully clean up.

more to the rhythm of the child, as well as to be more attentive to the Holy Spirit. Furthermore, material-making is an invaluable opportunity for us as adults to experience the integration of hand, mind, and heart.

Chapter 4

The Meaning, Importance, and Limitations of Our Catechetical Materials

The most important part of our work is to give the announcement (kerygma). So the catechetical materials not only have a pedagogical function, but they are also the instruments and means that allow us catechists to give the announcement. The materials themselves distinguish the Catechesis of the Good Shepherd and reflect the methodological character of our work.

The subject of materials might seem too simple and even unimportant, for it has to do with objects—little things, doll-like figurines—that do not compare to the Mystery, or the true material that is the Word of God. What is beautiful about our material is that, even though it is simple in nature, it serves as an instrument of knowledge of the Mystery.

Why do we need to think of a method and a material when the Church has already given us its own methodology and "material" in the liturgy? What purpose is served by an additional material, or one might say a sub-material, which could seem to be useless or even a hindrance?

We can only find the answer to these questions as we turn our eyes to the children, toward their deep needs in each developmental stage, the particular way they enter into vital contact with reality, and how we place ourselves in relationship to them. Also, in the religious arena, we need to keep in mind the stages of development articulated by Maria Montessori. Here I am referring to Montessori's four planes of development (see chapter 10) and specifically to the first two: zero to six years of age (infancy or early childhood), and six to twelve years of age (childhood). These two developmental periods have different characteristics. The first is more sensorial, while the second is more abstract and reflective. The differences in the two phases help clarify what distinguishes between religious sentiment and religious education.

Religious sentiment is a manifestation of the natural development of the child. The development of religious sentiment is akin to the development of senses, language, and movement, and is spurred from within the child. Religious education is the task of the educator, who draws from the heritage of culture and tradition, selecting and presenting what is most appropriate according to the developmental stage of the child. We already know very well how important it is to know who the child is in each developmental stage and how critical our own formation as catechists is. As catechists, we need to be well prepared in the areas of doctrine, pedagogy, and methodology.

The Role of the Materials

Everything that is placed in the environment is an instrument of education, whether directly or indirectly: the space itself, the persons who are there, and everything in the room, including the furniture and all decorative, utilitarian, and didactic objects that are found there.[1] First, let us focus on the materials that are specifically designed for the education of the children: materials in the strict sense of the word—structured, didactic material and sensorial materials. We seek here to deepen our understanding of the specific nature of the materials we use in the atrium.

In the marketplace we can find an infinite variety of materials: synthetic fibers, glass, metal, and so on, some of which never before existed. Modern technology has provided us with some of these, like plastics. We use these materials in our everyday lives: in laboratories, in our homes and businesses, in our means of transportation, and in every area of life. The variety and number of materials that surround

1. [Editor's note:] For example, the space itself directly facilitates the child's education because it is where the child learns and works with materials. The space also indirectly facilitates the child's education with its welcoming colors and ample room for the child to work, and by the catechist limiting unnecessary or loud sounds and distracting decorations.

us multiply our opportunities for sensorial experience, and yet, at the same time, their very number tends to numb our perceptions as to their individual characteristics and differences.

The variety of new materials and media have made it possible to expand knowledge of reality through a form of nonverbal communication, in which the message is conveyed through graphic design, color, objects, and so on, thus producing a more sensorial form of communication. Today's world of communication engages all the senses. We might think about color-coding, graphic symbols, designs, and the like that are used in hospitals and museums, as well as on street signs and tourist maps. Children experience this sensorial form of communication in the world around them. They see it and often touch it, but it is not really intended for them; it does not necessarily help their understanding or educate them.

In the specific world of education and instruction, we now have many instruments that are used for communication with children: transparencies[2], drawings, objects, educational games, and so on, many of which are designed to teach a specific skill or impart specific knowledge. If we want to use these materials in a truly educational way, we must choose from among the many possible materials, and we must be clear about the purpose and proper use of each material.

Teaching Aids

Let us now consider structured teaching aids, many of which were produced from the educational experiences of various pedagogues, including Froebel, Decroly, *le sorelle* (the sisters) Agazzi, along with many other, more recent ones. The main objective of these teaching aids has been to make scholastic achievement easier for children rather than to develop children's natural capacities, senses, and movement. These aids elicit certain mental and educational processes in children and are intended to make the children more secure in the particular discipline under study. Furthermore, these structured material aids function primarily as tools for teachers in implementing their lessons.

2. [Editor's note:] Modern technology such as Smartboards, iPads, the internet, etc., can also be considered instruments to enhance the child's education and knowledge. Just as the instruments listed in the paragraph above, technological instruments also have a specific purpose in the educational sphere; educators must be clear about which materials are chosen and their proper usage.

The Developmental, Sensorial Materials of Maria Montessori

According to the Montessori method, the *Casa dei Bambini* ("Children's House") is the environment prepared by Maria Montessori for children 3 to 6 years of age. All the things that make up the environment—the furniture, decorations, and objects designed for practical life activities, as well as structured didactic materials—are instruments of education, whether directly or indirectly,[3] and favor the child's auto-education and independence.

Among the direct aids provided with these aims in mind are the developmental, sensorial materials. Through systematic, sensorial experiences with materials that are freely chosen by the child, the child's senses are developed and refined, and his or her capacities are prepared for other areas of learning, including reading, writing, and arithmetic. These materials are not designed for random exploration; rather, they have a focused aim and are to be used in a precise way. A well-trained teacher demonstrates their proper use to the child so that the child might then use them independently to maximum advantage.

The sensorial materials and the materials designed for the acquisition of culture differ substantially from the teaching aids we have referred to earlier. The sensorial materials are designed to develop the child's abilities rather than to ensure the acquisition of a particular piece of information. Above all, the sensorial materials are an aid to the child rather than to the teacher.

Montessori defined her sensorial material as being a sort of "alphabet" that gives the child the necessary tools for "reading" the environment. Thus, the sensorial materials guide the child in ordering and clarifying the various sensorial impressions accumulated from everyday experience in the environment. The child's use of the developmental, sensorial materials creates within him or her a certain mental order that serves as a guide in spontaneous work. These materials incite spontaneous repetition of the exercise and develop the child's powers of concentration through the manipulation of the material and observation of its physical characteristics, and the materials change according to the child's handling of them. Thus, we can say that the

3. See footnote 1.

sensorial material is an instrument of the child's relationship with the environment and an aid to the child's development.

Why can it be said that the sensorial material is scientific? The sensorial material is scientific because its development is the result of long, experimental studies involving the observation of the way the child reacts to and relates with reality. Furthermore, these sensorial materials possess certain important characteristics for the child's development.

First, each of these materials has a built-in control of error so that the child can work independently, without having to rely on the teacher for the discovery and correction of mistakes.

The second characteristic pertains to aesthetics. Although the furnishings and materials of the prepared environment are simple, they need to be carefully proportioned in size and weight for the child's ease in using them, and they need to be attractive. Their color, luminosity, and harmony of form must attract children and inspire them to want to work with the materials.

The third characteristic is that the developmental materials must engage the child in appropriate work; that is, they must require the child's use of motor skills according to his or her stage of development. Montessori said that the possibility the material has for holding the child's attention does not depend on being beautiful or luxurious but on the opportunity it offers for ordered, controlled movement. The materials must engage the child in a definitive, purposeful, and intelligent work.

Finally, there is the particularly important characteristic of the limitations of the developmental, sensorial materials. Montessori noted that this is a valuable criterion pedagogically, while also one that is little understood or appreciated. In our times, we can say this is even more true. Think of the vast number of toys on the market today, as well as their diversity and complexity. Yet the more objects we put before the children, the more likely the children will be confused and disinterested. When we speak of the limitations of the materials, we are referring not only to the number of materials we place in the environment but also to the specific activity that each material calls forth. Each material will have only one purpose and prescribed use. The material is structured to indicate to the child a particular and singular route, a direct and narrow pathway, guiding the work according to a predetermined aim.

The criteria of the limitations of the materials is integrated with another pedagogical criterion: the isolation of difficulty. This criterion applies not only to the developmental, sensorial materials but also to the teacher's verbal presentation of a subject, in which the possibilities for confusing or complicating the subject for the child are many. Thus, the criterion of isolating the difficulty serves as a guide both in the *Casa dei Bambini* and in the elementary class.

Materials that Aid the Religious Formation of the Child

The catechetical materials have a dimension that is different from the Montessori developmental materials, rising primarily from their differing aims. The catechetical materials are not designed for the acquisition of some specific piece of knowledge concerning an aspect of concrete reality. Rather, the material helps the child foster a relationship, a living encounter with a real Person. Therefore, we can say that the primary aim of the catechetical material is to aid meditation and prayer while also honoring the vital needs and ways of learning that correspond to the child in his or her particular stage of development.

Certainly, then, the catechetical materials foster learning, but, above all, they are an aid to the child's religious life. To this end, various elements are incorporated in the making of the catechetical materials—sensorial elements as well as those that are more specifically doctrinal. The catechetical materials are a concrete means of transmitting the Word of God for the child so that the child can come to know that Person who has spoken in the Bible and is present to us in the liturgy.

Several of our catechetical materials have come to us directly from the work of Maria Montessori and from her experience of religious education with children, which she began in Barcelona in 1915. These include the model altar and articles of the Mass, the liturgical colors material and the liturgical calendar, along with the explanation of the Mass for children and their corresponding work of copying their own missal (which Montessori referred to as "The Open Book").

Our other catechetical materials have been the fruit of our observation of and experience with children in our Rome center over the years, confirmed by the responses of many children in various countries and from a wide variety of socioeconomic backgrounds. Some of these materials, such as the Unity Strip and the Plan of God, are religious adaptations of materials Montessori developed for children in the regular elementary class (not the atrium).

Maria Montessori's Work in Religious Education

Before proceeding with our discussion of catechetical materials, let us return for a moment to Montessori's early experience in the religious education of children. Responding to the call of Pope Pius X for the reform of religious education and the inclusion of younger children in the liturgical life of the Church, in 1915 Montessori created the first "atrium," which was connected to a Montessori school in Barcelona. The story of her experiences is told in the book *The Child in the Church* and is worthwhile reading.

Montessori describes the interest of a certain missionary priest, Father Casulleras of the Order of St. Vincent de Paul, in her Children's House, and their ensuing relationship. This relationship was instrumental in prompting her to think about the importance of the child being truly at home in the Church, which spurred her to apply her method directly to religious education.

What was novel in the arena of religious education was the fact that Montessori began with the youngest children. As Montessori tells it, "Formerly, when teaching was limited to telling the child the facts of sacred history and making him memorize, in catechism answers, the truths of Christian doctrine, we were, if I may be allowed so to express myself, drawing the child away from the church." The notion of renovating religious education for older children and teens was indicated by the reforms of Pius X,[4] but never before had it been considered to include children of three, four, and five years of age.

The abbot primate of the Sanctuary of Our Lady of Montserrat welcomed this idea and invited Anna Maccheroni, one of Montessori's collaborators, to speak at the Liturgical Congress taking place at the basilica of Montserrat in 1915. Presenting to all the clergy of Catalonia, Maccheroni stated in her presentation "The Liturgy and the Pedagogical Teaching of the Liturgy" (*Report of the Liturgical Congress of Montserrat*) that several aspects of the new catechetical directives proposed by Pius X could be applied to children of three, four, and five years of age. The proposal of Maccheroni, a woman of great faith in God and in the child, was accepted, and she was commissioned to proceed with its implementation in the Montessori School of the Barcelona Deputation. The first Children's House in the Church opened its doors on March 1, 1915, and, as Montessori noted, "it would remain a historical document of our work in education."

The Materials

As with any material, our catechetical material makes no sense and does not fulfill its purpose if it is not used properly by catechists who are well prepared. As we have often said before, the verbal meditation we offer in introducing a theme is indispensable, for it prepares for the hearing of God's Word, and the proclamation of God's Word is the primary task of the catechist; it is the moment of the objective presentation of the message. But the material helps the child ponder the Word; through repetition in working with the material, the child listens to that Word again and again for himself or herself and makes it his or her own.

In her book *Psychogeometry*, Montessori says, "Our education is an education from the periphery."[5] This splendid definition is valid for

4. His weekly catechism lessons in the courtyard of San Damaso in the Vatican always included a special place for children, and his decision to require the Confraternity of Christian Doctrine in every parish was partly motivated by a desire to save children from religious ignorance. See Steven M. Avella and Jeffrey Zalar, "Sanctity in the Era of Catholic Action: The Case of St. Pius X," *Catholic Historian* (Spirituality and Devotionalism edition) 15, no. 4 (Fall 1997): 57–80.

5. Maria Montessori, *Psychogeometry* (Amsterdam: Montessori-Pierson Publishing Company, 2011), chapter 1. This book was first published in 1934 in Barcelona, Spain. This English translation is based on Montessori's Italian manuscript as well as the 1934 Spanish edition.

general education, but it is all the more valid when applied to religious education. Montessori goes on to say that this education from the periphery replaces the old way of directing educational endeavors toward "the center." The center (the core of the child's being) is left alone so that natural energies might work together freely in the child's development. Furthermore, it is not necessary that we know the child's inner being; neither should we expect nor demand predetermined responses from the center. Rather, we must respect this innermost being of the child. We must render discreet service, both to the child and to God's Word.

Sofia Cavalletti states so eloquently in chapter 2 of *The Religious Potential of the Child* that nothing belongs to the adult, neither what he transmits, nor the soul of the child. They belong to God. They are gifts God gives because of his goodness and for our joy.[6] We would do well to ponder these words of wisdom and to be guided by them in how we conduct ourselves as catechists. Can we see, then, that the materials and the prepared environment offer us the means of educating from the periphery, and that they are a help to the child, a help that reaches the child's center,[7] which we do not need to know but do need to respect?

We have said that our material must not be a didactic aid, because it must not function as an aid to the teacher in getting the child to understand the lesson. Rather, if it is used properly, the catechetical material will be an aid to children's personal meditation. It will be the instrument that allows children to reflect on the Word of God for themselves, enabling them to pass from objectivity in considering that Word to subjectivity in the encounter with the Speaker, the true Teacher.

The material helps the catechist only in allowing him or her to observe the children, to see what they are drawn to, and to recognize particular interests, according to their developmental stages. An example would be the younger child's repetitive work with the Parable of the Good Shepherd materials. After proclaiming God's Word, the catechist shows the material, using only minimal movements in simple

6. Sofia Cavalletti, *The Religious Potential of the Child* (Chicago: Catechesis of the Good Shepherd Publications, 2020), chapter 2.

7. Cavalletti, *The Religious Potential of the Child*, chapters 1 and 2.

adherence to the text. The catechist does not impose personal feelings or reflections on the children in how she or he handles the material (such as patting the sheep on their heads, for example). The material is then offered for the child's personal work. The catechist does not intervene, except when the child requests that the catechist reread the text while the child moves the figures, or in those rare cases when the child might need to be stopped from inappropriate use of the material.

The catechetical material helps the child "see" the mystery of God hidden therein in much the same way that the liturgical signs and the parables communicate this mystery. What is concrete and perceivable through the senses becomes a vehicle that transports us to transcendent reality, a reality that is at the same time both revealed and hidden. Because we are given glimpses of this reality and find ourselves to be part of it, we can say it is "revealed." Yet because it is incommensurable and thus beyond us, we must also say it is "hidden." The materials are concrete aids for knowing the language, places and time of the Mystery of God, which children will take in and make their own according to their capacities and the rhythm of learning and development. With due respect for the differences, we can say that the catechetical material does what the liturgy does. Our relationship with God is largely built through concrete, sensory experience. This is a deep, vital need of the human being, and God honors this need by communicating with us through what is perceivable: through creation, through events in salvation history, through the Person of the Son, the Word, and God's continued presence in the sacraments. Thus, a concrete, perceivable "material" is always involved in God's self-communication to us.

Liturgy employs this same method of communication that we refer to as the "method of signs," in which the "materials" are the water, bread, wine, and so on. Likewise, the parables of Jesus also "hide" the Mystery in elements of everyday life—for example, seeds growing in fields, yeast causing the bread to rise. The Mystery requires a material element in order to be perceived. This is true for both the adult and the child. It is for this reason that we prepare materials for the children, and also for this reason that our making of the material is also a help to our own penetration of the Mystery.

As catechists of the Good Shepherd, we all know how important it is that we present and use the materials well. And we know that this requires of us a thorough preparation and ongoing formation if we are to grow in our ability to assist the child in his or her relationship with God with ever increasing respect, sensitivity, and knowledge.

Chapter 5

The Three-Period Lesson

The three-period lesson is a technique that Montessori adapted from her earliest experiences with children and used for each presentation in the Children's House[1]. We apply this technique in catechesis because it respects the stages of the child's psychological maturation. Why three periods? Because there are three moments of learning. The following example will illustrate the technique of the three-period lesson using the naming of the chalice, which is part of the presentation of the articles of Mass.

First Period

Aim: Associating the sensorial perception of the object with its name.

- We present the object to the child and say, "This is the chalice."
- We offer a simple identification concerning its use: "It holds the wine at Mass."
- We repeat the name of the object without its article: ("Chalice,") pronouncing the word very clearly.

We are careful not to say more, because what is important is that the name is linked to the object in the child's consciousness.

Second Period

Aim: Recognizing the object corresponding to the name.

- With several of the model articles of Mass visible to the child, we ask, "Which one is the chalice?"
- In pronouncing the name, we are offering a mnemonic help to the child, who will point to the chalice. The child has then associated the object with its name.

1. Maria Montessori, *The Discovery of the Child*, The Montessori Series, vol. 1 (Amsterdam: Montessori-Pierson Publishing, reprinted 2019), 168–170.

A great deal of attention must be given to the mnemonic and associative exercise of the second period. We can repeat the question on many occasions during subsequent presentations of the model altar as well as just after the child has set up the model altar for himself or herself. Repeating this exercise of association enables the child to learn the object's name and fix it in his or her memory.

The catechist must be alert to whether the child has yet truly taken in the presentation. If the child cannot immediately point to the object being named, it is a signal to the catechist to discontinue the exercise. The catechist does not correct the child; instead, the catechist repeats the first-period lesson at a later time.

Third Period

Aim: Remembering the name corresponding to the object.

- We place the object before the child and ask: "What is this?"
- If the child answers readily, it is a verification of the child's absorption and a certain maturation, indicating that the goals of the first and second periods have been accomplished.

The catechist should wait to do the third period until he or she is reasonably sure the child is capable of answering correctly. If in doubt, then the adult must continue repeating the first and second periods. Often the third period is a long time in coming. We must remember that maturation of learning varies in each individual. It is important not to rush the third period. If we ask the child too soon "What is this?" we risk humiliating the child who is not yet capable of answering correctly.

Without being aware they are doing it, adults often are engaging in a three-period lesson with young children even before they can talk. For example, every time a mother says to her child "Here is your nose" and "Where is your nose?" she is doing the first and second periods. She is helping the child to recognize something and to learn its name. The child associates object and name even if he or she is unable to talk.

The three periods are an essential element in almost all presentations, even with children over six years, and need not be limited to lessons of nomenclature. Another way of looking at the three periods is as corollaries to the three moments of learning:

- In the first period or moment, one is put in contact with the subject.

- In the second period, one engages in an activity or, in some way, interacts with the subject, which helps one's absorption of the subject and aids mental retention.
- In the third period, one achieves a degree of ownership of the subject; the subject has become clear enough or enough a part of oneself so that he or she can say something about it and can also communicate the subject to others.

We see these three moments of learning going on in the atrium all the time. In the first period, we put the child in contact with some specific part of their environment or some specific part of the Christian proclamation. In presentations of the Word or liturgy, the meditative questions we pose, though often unanswered in the moment, are a start toward the second period. The child begins to ponder or to interact with the subject.

The child's choice of and work with the catechetical material following a presentation brings about the fullest entry into the second period.

The child's having arrived at the third period or moment of learning is often evidenced in their artwork or in their spontaneous comments. Moreover, it is interesting to note that arriving at the third period also involves a particular capacity to synthesize, to make connections with other subjects, and to see the interconnectedness of certain subjects.

The three-period lesson might seem, at least at first glance, to be a dry technique or too calculated. Yet it turns out to be, just as Montessori indicated, valid and effective for all nomenclature with children from 3 to 6 years of age. Besides leading to understanding of the subject being presented, the three-period lesson is a reminder to us that in all communications, even with older children, it is important to speak in a simple way. We need to use few words, presenting the subject objectively, just as it is, and resist the urge to add our own embellishments and reflections. The essentiality of the child requires this discipline from us. In the words of Maria Montessori, "The teacher should avoid the superfluous, but should not forget the necessary. The superfluous and the lack of the necessary are the two chief errors of the teacher; the line of demarcation between the two indicates the level of the teacher's perfection."[2]

2. Montessori, *The Discovery of the Child*, 177.

Chapter 6

Organization of a Catechetical Center

What distinguishes catechetical centers is how they are set up according to the local culture and the availability of space and funds. What is consistent in all catechetical centers, however, is that the prepared environments respect the developmental needs of the child. As we have discovered in our work in the centers in Italy, there are certain consistent factors beyond culture, space, and financial resources that help the catechist create a special environment for the children. The catechist creates not only the physical environment, but also, more importantly, the catechist must create a spiritual one. This spiritual environment should be conducive to helping both the children and the adults within that environment to be attentive and responsive to God's presence.

The original atrium in Rome

The environment of the Catechesis of the Good Shepherd, which we call the *atrium*, is not a school. It is a place of religious experience, one that is shared by adults and children. The adults present have the practical task of preparing the environment and assisting the children's work within that environment. Furthermore, all the adults involved in the catechesis take on specific tasks after discernment of individual abilities and interests, as well as training and experience.

Collaborating with Parents

In addition to forming the groups of children according to the developmental periods of 3 to 6 years, 6 to 9 years, and 9 to 12 years of age, and deciding on the appropriate spaces for each group, the catechist should try to get to know the parents before beginning the atrium year. This will be a help to the child and his or her experience in the atrium.

Also, the parents need help to understand the child's experience in the atrium and the importance and nature of the child's relationship with God. This is best accomplished through regular parent education sessions in which the parents receive some of the same presentations their children are receiving in the atrium, as well as through regular parent conferences.

Often the children reflect at home on what they have heard or done in the atrium, and the parents feel unable to respond appropriately. Thus, we will share with them how the spiritual riches of the child are developed in the atrium and how they are manifested in an atmosphere of order and trust, especially through the child's personal work. We will also advise the parents of the importance of the child's regular attendance and punctual arrival at the atrium. Finally, it is very important that these communications with the parents be kept separate from the atrium sessions so that the children know that, when they come to atrium, this is their time and that the catechist is fully available to them.

Once the children have settled into the atrium and are well established in their work, parents might be invited (one at a time) to come and observe. It is helpful to prepare them in advance for this experience, particularly to encourage them to be as unobtrusive a presence as possible so that they do not distract their own child or other children from their work.

The catechist establishes the yearly calendar for the atrium in consultation with the parents and appropriate parish staff. It is best not to begin the atrium year at the same time as the start of the children's school year, as they need time settle into each environment separately.

Also, it is important that the atrium sessions be scheduled so that they do not conflict with the families' attendance at Mass. For example, if the parish atrium meets on Sundays, there are two important considerations to keep in mind: (1) the atrium session needs to end in time for the children to join their families for the Liturgy of the Eucharist, and (2) the children need much more time in the atrium than is allowed during the Liturgy of the Word portion of Mass. Practically speaking, this means that if the atrium is held on Sunday morning, schedule it to begin well before the start of Mass; the children need up to two hours in the atrium in order to engage fully in their chosen work. For this reason, atrium sessions are often scheduled on Saturdays or weekday afternoons.

Before the Children Come

The catechist keeps a record of the name, age, home address, parents' names and phone numbers, emergency contacts, and any other information that will help the catechist meet the needs of the child. It is also useful to note when presentations are given to the child and to record some of the child's comments and particular interests as revealed by the child's chosen work in the atrium.

As a rule, the catechist should arrive at the atrium well before the children in order to care for the environment. The catechist checks the materials and overall order of the atrium calmly and peacefully before each session as part of his or her preparation to be fully present, both to the children and to God during the atrium session. The room arrangement and furnishings must accommodate the children's freedom of movement within the environment. The materials must be complete and well maintained to invite and facilitate the work of the children. Furthermore, the materials each have their own fixed place on a shelf and should not be moved unless the child's work requires them to.

It is a good practice for the catechists and assistants to gather after each atrium session to share evaluations and reflections of that day and to celebrate the experience. This time would also be an opportunity to plan for the next session.

How to Begin with a Group of Children

At the beginning of the atrium year, it is necessary to help the children

- orient themselves to the environment in order to make it their own,
- practice focused, controlled movements (of particular importance for the younger children), and
- correctly use the objects and materials in order to (*a*) achieve independence and concentration in their work, and (*b*) learn to respect the independence and concentration of the other children.

If the group of younger children is large, we might have four or five children come to the atrium at a time for the first three or four weeks. Once the separate groups are acclimated to the environment, the whole group can be formed.

Also, for very young children we begin with shorter sessions of forty-five minutes to an hour and gradually increase the time to two or two-and-a-half hours. The longer amount of time will become essential in order for them to enter fully into the rhythm of the atrium. This rhythm usually includes a time for gathering and settling, a short presentation (the time of the Christian Proclamation), a substantial time to work, a time for the children to put their things away and restore the environment without rushing, and finally a time to gather as a group and end the day together with song and prayer.

From the first meetings with the children, it will be important to establish certain norms of behavior in the atrium, such as how we speak (in a soft voice), how we move (carefully, not to disturb others), and so on. In the atrium we will have only a few rules, but these rules will be firmly observed. It is not strange to the children, nor should it be to us adults, that such a special place, where one is to meet God in a particular way, requires of us distinct ways of moving, speaking, and interacting with one another.

In the beginning we need to present these behavioral practices to the children in a formal way. Later, as the children become accustomed to the environment and are self-directed in their work, these behaviors tend to become second nature.

In the atrium there is no large teacher's desk occupying the front center of the room. Instead, the catechist will have a small chair and table like those of the children, situated in an area of the room that allows the catechist to observe the children and makes the catechist easily accessible to the children who may come to him or her for help.

For the Christian Proclamation, which is made each time the children come to the atrium, it is customary to have the children bring their own chairs to form a circle. (How to carry a chair is one of the early movement lessons. See chapter 7.) Sometimes, for solemn celebrations or special presentations, it can be helpful for the children to find their chairs already arranged.

For some individual or small-group presentations, the children gather where the material that interests them is displayed (such as near the model altar or the baptism area). Other presentations require that the catechist bring a material to a table (such as the infancy narratives, the parables of the kingdom).

For their personal work the younger children like to be seated at a small (individual-sized) table, or else they will spread a small rug or mat on the floor on which to place their work. For this reason, one of the rules of the atrium will be to walk carefully around the mats, not to disturb the other children's work.

Finally, with a group of younger children, there are three particular areas we focus on in the beginning: controlled movement, practical life activities, and silence exercises. In a Montessori Children's House these areas of work with the children are fundamental because they place in clear harmonious relationship the "I" of the child and the child's external reality. Furthermore, in the atrium the children become aware that the ability to control themselves, to perfect themselves, and to live harmoniously with others directly serves their relationship with God.

In an atrium that is part of a Montessori Children's House it is not necessary to focus as much on formal lessons in these areas, because they form part of the child's daily school life. Still, it is important to note that in the atrium the children seem to find the fullest meaning or expression of what they have learned in the regular Montessori environment.

In these areas of controlled movement, practical life, and silence exercises we are given a further opportunity to observe the children and to discern how best to help them in their personal development. Furthermore, each of the areas of controlled movement, practical life, and silence plays its part in the creation of the atrium environment, in the work of the children and in the overall atmosphere of concentration, meditation, and prayer. These areas are so important that we have addressed them in separate sections later in this book (see chapters 7 and 15).

Chapter 7

Welcoming the Children

The First Day

It is important in working with the children to begin in the right way from the very first meeting. The catechist will have already prepared by getting to know the children and their families. He or she will also have carefully prepared the environment for the children, as well as himself or herself to be with the children and God in the atrium. The following are some suggestions for the catechist to help the children become acclimated to the atrium environment and for the atrium community to organize itself.

If possible, we will choose a gathering space near but outside the atrium. Here we will greet the children and invite them to sit down. While waiting for the other children to arrive we engage them in simple conversation to get acquainted with one another. During this gathering time we also invite them to put themselves in physical order (hands clean, hair combed, shoes tied, and so on). These formalities are not always necessary, but they underline the importance of the encounter.

We name the place they have come to as the atrium, and we identify it as a place specially prepared for us to come to know God better.

Then, calling each child by name in a whisper, we invite them to enter the atrium and choose a chair on which to sit. (We might show them how to carry their own chair to the circle, or we might have the chairs already placed in a circle.)

Once all are seated, we point out to them some of the different areas of the atrium, such as the model altar, the baptism corner, the geography, and infancy narrative area that help us learn about Jesus' birth, and so on. We give special emphasis to the prayer corner.

We continue our introduction to the atrium: "Why have we come here? What will we do here? Talk about God, listen to God, work, sing, and pray are some things we will do here to come to know God better."

In this first encounter we will go on to demonstrate some of the ways we will move and act in this special place. These kinds of demonstrations will be done every time the children come to the atrium, especially in the early weeks. The demonstrations will help the children become familiar with the environment and function comfortably within it. For the first day we are sure to include how to speak softly and move slowly and carefully, how to greet one another, where to get a drink or where the restroom is, and so on.

Our time together most often ends at the prayer corner. Depending on the readiness of the group, we might prepare the prayer table together on the first day, making a simple procession to carry the articles for the table: the appropriately colored cloth (which is usually green, since we begin the atrium year in Ordinary Time before Advent), the Bible, candles, perhaps a sacred image, and some flowers.

At the prayer corner we light the candles and perhaps read a short Psalm phrase. After a brief time of silence, prayer, and a song we say goodbye to one another, and the children go home.

The dismissal time needs to be conducted in the same quiet, orderly way as the rest of the atrium session. The catechist might remain with the children at the prayer table singing, while an assistant signals quietly to the catechist as each parent arrives, and the catechist in turn dismisses the respective child. This method of dismissal is often preferable, as it avoids the potential restlessness of children who have to stand around and wait for parents who might be late. Otherwise, the catechist might take all the children together to the place where the parents will pick them up.

All these formalities help us begin a good work with the children. We will perhaps be surprised at how much self-discipline the children are capable of having and how happy they are to have it. Respect for the rules of behavior, which we call forth from the first day will help create an atmosphere of work that favors meditation and prayer. Note that in subsequent years there will be less of a need on our part to teach the formalities, because the children who are already acclimated to the environment will teach the new children.

Movement Exercises[1]

The movement exercises, or lessons of controlled movement, help the children gain control of their bodies and correctly use the things in the environment. The following are some of the movements the catechist might demonstrate in the early weeks of the atrium sessions:

- How to carry a chair
- How to sit
- How to roll out and put away a floor mat
- How to walk around the mats placed on the floor (where another child might be working)

Gianna with a group of children in the original Rome Atrium

The catechist demonstrates these movements slowly and deliberately, using few words. The aim is to make the movement itself visible and clear to the child, so that he or she can readily repeat it. If done well, these movement lessons are very pleasing and interesting to the children. In addition to helping the child gain independence and self-confidence, they help establish the behavioral practices that are necessary for the smooth functioning of the atrium community. The catechist will need to decide the specific movement exercises that are called for according to the particular physical and social characteristics of the atrium.

Showing the children how to move is the key to obtaining discipline and order in the group. The more movements that are

1. To gain a deeper understanding of the importance of the movement exercises, one is advised to read in Montessori's books: *The Secret of Childhood,* chapter 15, "Movement"; *The Discovery of the Child,* chapter 6, "Education in Movement"; and *The Absorbent Mind,* chapter 13, "The Importance of Movement and General Development." In these chapters Montessori stresses the importance of movement in the psychic makeup of the child and in the development of life in human society.

demonstrated, the more we advance toward the goal of facilitating an orderly expansion of the small child's activity. So let the catechist present all those movements of daily life, such as moving a chair, standing up and sitting down, offering an object to another person, opening the door, letting someone pass by, picking up and setting down objects, gathering things that have fallen and replacing them carefully, and so on.

The movement exercises, harmoniously uniting mind and muscles, prepare the way to self-control, the possession of free will, and a natural obedience. They lead to concentration and finally to meditation, which forms the basis of prayer. Thus, the control of movements that can be gained through these exercises is of enormous help to the child.

It is important, however, that we do not interpret these exercises as having the limited objective of maintaining discipline and order in the class. These exercises correspond to a deep, vital need in the child for order. They give the child a sense of self-mastery, and thus self-confidence, calling him or her to repetition of the exercise and to greater concentration.

The importance of movement in religious formation is perhaps best expressed in the prayer of a particular child in the atrium: "My body is happy!" It is also necessary for us as adults to control our movements and gestures, especially in order to be centered and focused in prayer. Thus, we too are helped by the movement exercises.

Practical Life Activities

Often when the children come to the atrium, they bring some flowers. We take the opportunity to show them how to arrange the flowers in a vase and place them on the prayer table or at some chosen spot in the atrium. Flower arranging is among many other works that Montessori referred to as "practical life activities." These activities have to do with the care of one's person and the care of the environment.

In a Montessori Children's House, the children spend a good amount of time on these activities. Practical life activities offer the opportunity for intelligent work. They correspond to the child's need for movement, order, and independence. For this reason, it is very important that we adults not view the practical life activities merely as the duty or personal responsibility of the child in helping to keep the environment in good order. Rather, we must understand that the practical life activities fulfill a deep need in the child (especially in the younger child) and are directly connected to the religious life of the child.

Knowing how to use objects correctly, how to carry things, how to care for one's surroundings, and so on, all share an aim that goes beyond physical functioning. Both the movement exercises and the practical life activities nurture wholeness in the child. The children carry out these activities with joy. They live a religious experience in the totality of their persons.

We have all noted how very young children want to participate in the activities they see adults doing. Why? These activities are part of the daily life of every child since birth. Just as the child absorbs language, so does the child absorb the actions or activities of the culture surrounding him or her, particularly those which are carried out in the daily life of the family.

The child of only one or two years has already begun observing and absorbing these practical life activities. He or she has already begun to understand the meaning of some objects and their use and is able to associate the objects with the people who use them. The young child even has rudimentary control of his or her own movements and is trying to participate in the family's activities. The child is no longer satisfied just to watch these activities going on; rather, he or she now has an irresistible urge to do the activities as they correspond to a vital need within. The child wants to repeat and to accomplish the task for the profound and internal satisfaction of improvement. In the process of doing the task, in both the repetition of the task and its accomplishment, the child builds his or her own sense of security. When the adult prevents the work, interrupts it, or interferes in it, the adult distracts the child from his or her normal path of development. The work of the adult, therefore, is that of creating the conditions that are conducive to the child's development.

As the child continues to absorb the surroundings, the child begins to imitate adults and, with great effort, progresses toward the ability to master the environment. In her book *The Absorbent Mind,* in the chapter on "Development and Imitation," Montessori writes:

"The important thing is that before the child can imitate, he must be prepared for doing so, and this preparation derives from the effort he has been making."[2]

The child carries out the practical life exercises not just because they are useful, but also because, through them, the child experiences the profound internal satisfaction of growing in independence and of integrating intelligence, will, and movement. Indirectly, these activities help to consolidate and develop coordination of movements through experience and much repetition. Children want and need to occupy themselves with these activities. Furthermore, they want to do them alone, because the activity has as its aim a work, and the work has as its aim independence. Children have a natural drive toward independence and ask of us, however indirectly or even silently, "Help me do it myself."

Practical life activities are not limited to domestic tasks, such as cleaning and other household jobs that serve individual human life. These activities have a broader aim in that they involve work in the service of others. We can set forth the principle that human work does not have the singular purpose of survival and physical well-being. Rather, in those who believe, work becomes a service that transcends them. It becomes service to God.

Recalling her first experience in the field of religious formation of children in Barcelona, Maria Montessori said that the children manifested a new dignity and joy in performing practical life activities within a religious environment. It was as if, in that particular environment, they had found the purpose of all they had practiced in school.

The Presentation of Practical Life Activities

The catechist first names the activity (pouring, dusting, plant leaf cleaning, and so on) and then does the exercise slowly and with deliberate movements. The catechist uses few or no words, so as not to confuse the two languages of gesture and word. When the presentation is for a group of children, two or three children are invited to then repeat the exercise in front of the others. Afterward, each child is offered the opportunity to repeat the exercise as many times as he or she wants

2. Maria Montessori, *The Absorbent Mind*, The Montessori Series, vol. 1 (Amsterdam: Montessori-Pierson Publishing, reprinted 2019), 141.

during the individual work time. The catechist will not interfere in the child's work in order to correct a mistake. Rather, if the catechist notes that the child continues to make mistakes, he or she will ask, "Do you know how to do this?" The child may not even be capable of answering the question. The catechist will then re-present the exercise at a later time, with distinct movements done in succession, without interrupting the action. Obviously, not all the children can be invited to do the same activity at the same time. The children learn that we do not all have the same tasks. They learn to choose their own work.

Materials for practical life activities

Arranging Flowers in a Vase

Description of the Material: If there is not a surface or work area in the environment set aside specifically for flower arranging, then you may prepare the following items on a tray, which can be carried to a table for the work:

- a plastic cloth the size of a small table
- a collection of small vases from which the child may choose
- a pitcher of water
- a small basin (preferably made of clear glass)
- a funnel (for pouring water into the smaller vases)
- a good pair of small scissors
- a little towel
- a bucket

Presentation: First we name for the child what we are going to do. Then we spread the cloth on the table and begin placing the items on the cloth in order, starting from the left. The flowers themselves are placed in front of the other items. We put the funnel into the vase and fill the vase with water. We pour the rest of the water into the basin. The towel is used to wipe up any drips from the pitcher.

The stems of the flowers are submerged in the basin of water. Next, we cut each stem one by one according to the height of the vase. Then, we discard the stem clippings and leaves into the bucket. We carry the flowers in their vase to their chosen place in the atrium. Finally, we return the flower-arranging materials to their place, wiping up the cloth and table as needed.

Other Practical Life Activities in the Atrium

Practical life activities might vary across atriums, depending on their particular space. For instance, in an atrium with low windows, a favorite practical life activity might be that of cleaning windows. Basic practical life activities that would be found in almost any atrium include: sweeping, dusting, cleaning a table, plant care (such as watering or leaf cleaning), pouring (particularly the filling of the water and wine cruets), and polishing. (The younger children especially enjoy polishing the brass articles used on the model altar).

Artwork and Handwork

As previously noted, after the catechist gives the Christian Proclamation (the presentation from the Scriptures or the liturgy), the children are invited to choose a work. They may work with a specific catechetical material or engage in a practical life activity. The children might also choose artwork (such as free drawing or painting) or other handwork (such as pasting, tracing, or template work). For these works, we prepare a shelf that is easily identifiable and accessible with all the necessary materials.

Materials for artwork and handwork

Through our demonstration of the correct use of the art and handwork materials, the aims of the lessons in art and handwork are

- to give the child further access to and knowledge of the environment,
- to invite controlled movement, which leads to greater concentration, and
- to offer the child the opportunity, through the work of their hands, to continue their meditation and reflection on the Christian Proclamation.

Creative artwork (or free drawing, painting, and so on) is an important way that the children ponder and respond to the Christian Proclamation in the atrium. Thus, we provide a few simple, but good quality art materials. We demonstrate the use of these materials, and we invite the children to draw something they have seen or experienced in the atrium. This invitation is made at the outset of the atrium year and is continually made throughout the year as a work the child might choose following the Christian Proclamation.

Two of the handworks that the children often choose in the atrium are pasting and tracing. Although the children will do these works independently, these handworks may be presented to a small group. The catechist names the activity, showing the children where the corresponding materials are kept on the shelf and then carrying the materials to a small table. The catechist arranges the materials on the table and carefully demonstrates the activity. When the work is finished the materials will be returned to their place on the shelf. The child will put his or her work in a personal folder. This gives the child an opportunity to complete unfinished work at a later time, if he or she so chooses.

Pasting

This is a very simple activity that is presented early in the atrium year. The work is interesting and easy to do, even for children as young as three years old. Children this age might not know how to handle a pencil yet, but they can manage a pasting brush. For this activity we provide a pasting set that includes

- a small container of paste, which the child can easily open,
- a small paste brush,

- a small piece of cloth (for wiping off excess paste),
- a small tray for holding the articles listed above, and
- a mat or cardboard underlay on which to do the pasting work.

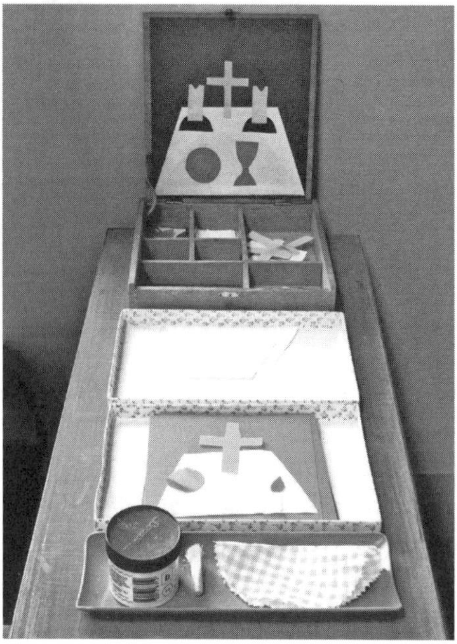
Materials for pasting

The pasting set is then used in conjunction with a box that has been prepared for collage work; the items for pasting might correlate to a particular theme or subject. An example of this kind of box is the one prepared for altar pasting. The child will find the cut-outs needed: paper chalices, patens, candles, and the crucifix, along with the paper altar cloths. The number of cut-outs corresponds to the number of children in the atrium.

Tracing

Tracing is not meant to supplant free drawing; still, it is an interesting and engaging handwork, especially for the child who has gained enough hand control to use a pencil and who is, simultaneously, learning to write. For this activity we provide

- tracing paper cut to fit over the tracing cards,
- #2 pencil,
- colored pencils (the number of colors is limited at first but will later increase), and
- large paper clips or a clipboard to secure the tracing paper to the tracing card.

Tracing packets are prepared according to the respective subject (such as "Articles of the Mass" or "Articles of Baptism," and so on). These packets contain designs, colored as well as outlined in black, on white cards that measure 20 × 20 cm (about 8 inches square) or 14 × 14 cm (about 5½ inches square).

Chapter 8

First Presentations to Introduce the Mass

The earliest presentations to introduce the Mass are lessons of nomenclature and movement. The material used for these lessons is a miniature altar (smaller than child-sized) with a small sacristy cabinet containing the articles used for Mass. These articles are proportionately sized to fit the small altar table.

The first presentation, given to 3-year-olds, focuses on the altar table, the altar cloth, the paten, the chalice, the candles, and the crucifix. The catechist names each article (stressing the name itself, and inviting the children to repeat the name), gives a brief identification of the article (for example: "This is the paten. It holds the bread for Mass."), and carefully places it on the altar table. When the catechist has finished naming and placing the articles, he or she lights the candles and makes the solemn proclamation: "Christ has died, but He is risen." The catechist then allows for the responses of the children (a few moments of silent enjoyment, or verbal reflections, or songs). The presentation closes with the catechist renaming each article as he or she carefully places it back in the sacristy cabinet, before inviting the children to choose their work. Later presentations of the miniature altar will focus on the tabernacle, the Word, and remaining articles of the Mass.

Miniature altar

The direct aim of these presentations is to name, identify, and make accessible the articles of Mass to the children. The corresponding primary work of the children is that of setting up the altar for themselves. They might also engage in practical life activities involving the model altar (such as polishing, candle-trimming, or laundering the cloths), or they might choose to do a handwork (such as pasting or tracing) or their own creative artwork. All of these works serve to deepen the child's familiarity with and enjoyment of the altar. They also invite and nurture controlled movement which, as we know, is an indirect preparation for prayer. (Please see the section in chapter 7 on movement exercises, page 47, and practical life, page 48, as well as the section in chapter 15 on controlled movement, page 103, related to prayer.)

Miniature altar with labels

Another important indirect aim of these presentations is to deepen the children's natural interest in and attraction to the church—to help them feel more at home in church and to participate more fully in the Mass (even before they are receiving the Eucharist). Thus, as we admire together the beauty of the articles during First Presentations to Introduce the Mass altar presentations, we are also saying that the actual articles (the ones of the church) are even more beautiful. Soon after we have given the presentation at the model altar and the children have begun their own work with it, we then take the children into the church to find and admire the actual altar and articles of Mass.

Sacristy cabinet

All of these early presentations of the altar have a character that may be described as "sensorial" because they stir the senses of sight, hearing, and touch. Sensory awareness is the base of all knowledge for the younger child. Furthermore, these first presentations satisfy a deep need for movement from the children. It has been demonstrated that movement is the realization of intelligence and a fundamental factor in the development of personality. Moreover, they are an essential preparation for later presentations on the Mass, which focus more directly on its core mysteries.

Chapter 9

The Two Lines of Education

Our task as catechists and as believers is a special one that resonates in our teaching and involves us as Christians and as educators. It is appropriate, therefore, to reflect on how Maria Montessori understood education.

Montessori presented the diagram, found below, at the International Course in Perugia, in 1950. It can serve as a guide in considering the educational process.

The top line is the line of personal development that goes from zero—indeed, it begins before birth—to age twenty-four. The bottom line represents education in the traditional school system—that is, education conceived as something the educator gives to the student. These two concepts of education do look to the same end: the actualization of the child's personality so that the individual can fulfill his or her own unique functions and roles in society.

The Two Lines of Education

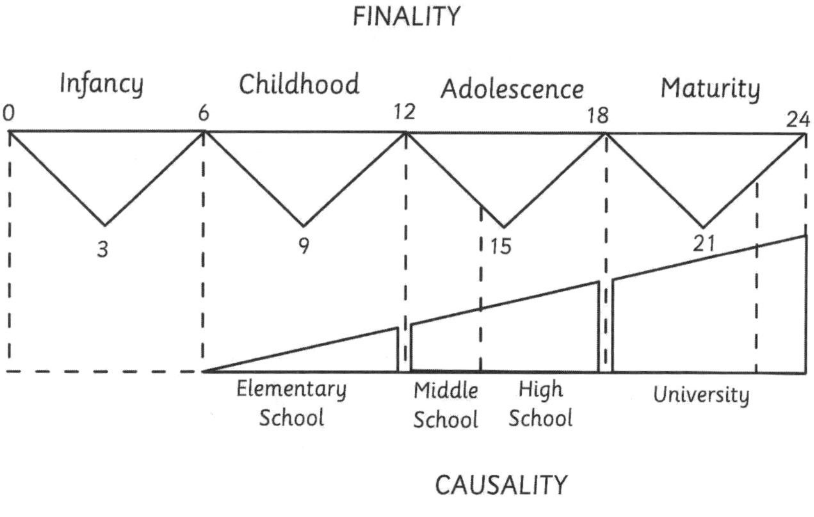

The top line clearly shows a regular progression. On the chronological lifeline are formed four triangles, which represent the four phases of human development recognized by modern psychology: infancy, childhood, adolescence, and maturity. The bottom line shows an educational process that begins only at age 6, when society normally begins to take the child into account.

Notice that on the bottom line the vertex of the triangle widens and progressively increases. This represents how the child's intelligence continually increases and, therefore, the degree of education must also continually increase. Also, notice that there is no continuity between the segments of the triangle on the bottom line. On the contrary, there is a clear division marking the jump from one segment to the next, from elementary school to middle school to high school and to college.

According to Montessori, the bottom line should correspond to the top line of life development. Yet all of us who have been involved in the traditional school system know how readily the focus is placed more on programs than on observing and responding to individual development. This diagram reminds us that traditional approach to education still has far to go in bringing the educational process into harmony with individual development.

Although these two concepts of education are very different, they do have points of contact, and they can be brought into agreement. This cannot happen, however, unless certain basic preconceptions about education are completely abolished.

Before going further with a discussion of the diagram, it would be useful to reflect on the word *education* and come to an understanding of its meaning. In an old Italian encyclopedia we read, "By this expression is generally understood the sum total of processes whereby any community or social group whatsoever transmits all that it possesses, in reality or in potential, for the purpose of ensuring its own continuity of existence and development" (P. Fedele, UTET, 1935).[1]

This definition indicates that all of life is an educational process, from childhood to maturity. Today, more than ever, adults are called to cultivate personality, character, and capabilities through constant

1. [Editor's note:] Though this definition comes from an old text, it clearly communicates Gianna's understanding of education.

and necessary contact with other people who have different training, cultural background, and habits. Adults must necessarily be involved with diverse social, cultural, and religious institutions. How is it then that, in common language, the word *education*, when used in the context of children, usually only refers to the action of the adult toward the growing child? In fact, adults themselves are continually being submitted to an educational process.

We are all on the same level in being educated by life itself and by each other (the concept of mutual education). It seems to me that this reality should bring us, as adults, to an attitude of greater attention and humility before others, including and especially the child! When this discussion is framed in pedagogical terms, it can help to eliminate one of the many prejudices that form the base of disharmony between the two lines of education, as indicated by the diagram. As adults and as educators we are not the ones who give rise to the process of development of the human being. Life itself does this according to its universal laws, even if these laws are not yet fully understood. This reality should compel adults to want to know the child and to find the best possible way of assisting the child's self-education.

Throughout the past century, significant discoveries and advancements have influenced the educational processes. Theorists are less inclined to view education as depending on external causes and laws that act on and develop the human being based on norms and goals imposed from the outside. Indeed, it was formerly presumed, with sincere conviction, that the process of a child's personality development was called forth by means of the education imparted by adults. Now, more and more, the value of freedom in the educational process is being recognized and affirmed. Educators today are more aware of and attentive to collaboration with those being educated. This means there is greater concern for nurturing the process of self-education.

Still, there remain so many contradictions, delays, and unsuccessful programs. What the adult world has yet to fully confront, and what particularly interests us as catechist-educators, is that the true personality of the child is still buried under prejudices that keep adults from seeing the child clearly. Our vision of the child is still obstructed by habit and traditional educational practices. Adults must place themselves in right relationship with the child, in a spirit of humility and respect, in order to learn the child's true nature and the universal laws that guide and determine his or her development.

Montessori wrote, "If we succeed only in proving the existence of these prejudices, we will already have given a benefit of general import,"[2] as well as "Children are for everyone empty beings for whom only play, sleep, and the pastime of fantasy tales are appropriate. A serious mental work in children so young seems a sacrilege. . . . As far as instruction is concerned, we worry about keeping the child from mental efforts and precocious intellectual applications."[3]

As to the child's physical development, adults tend to assume that young children are unable to control their movements. We manifest this misconception when we take on the tasks of dressing them, putting food in their mouths, and so on, thus hindering the children themselves from having those experiences that are essential in their quest for independence and self-confidence.

In short, we adults are often so focused on our role as educator that we forget to respect the child. If we were to reflect on our relationship with the child, at home or in society, we could verify the existence of these prejudices. Furthermore, if we apply these observations to the field of religious education, we find ourselves even more submerged in these prejudices.

The Church has always recognized the child's dignity as a child of God from the moment of conception and invites the newborn child to the sacrament of baptism. The Eastern Churches go so far as to offer newborns the Eucharist, thus viewing them as capable of participation in the most essential act of Christian life. But in spite of this understanding of the child's dignity, the Church still tends to wait until the child is six years of age to begin formal religious education. And even then the focus is more on religious *instruction* than on religious *formation*.

If we were to apply the diagram of "The Two Lines of Education" to the sphere of religious education, we would find an even greater contrast between the top and bottom lines. We would also find the same basic prejudices. It might be commonplace to think that serious

2. Maria Montessori, *Formation of Man*, The Montessori Series, vol. 3 (Amsterdam: Montessori-Pierson Publishing, reprinted 2019), 16.

3. Montessori, *Formation of Man*, 22.

theological concepts are incomprehensible to young children, even though experience has revealed that the link between God and the child is deeply rooted. Even from a very young age, the child has the capacity to see the invisible within the visible (or the transcendent within the perceivable). The young child has a capacity for living in profound rapport with God, which expresses itself in prayer.

It is precisely in the field of religious education that we should most readily pursue the full actualization of the child's potential and free ourselves from the traditional conception of education as something the adult gives to the child. It is precisely in this religious sphere that educational practices must be freed from external causality and must, instead, follow the "constructive rhythms of Life," if we are convinced that life comes from God.

From the beginning of her experiences in observing the child within a suitably prepared environment (1907), Maria Montessori discovered characteristics in the child that were completely new and previously unsuspected. This discovery of the child's true nature forms the basis of her work in education. What is often referred to as "the Montessori method" views education as "an aid to Life itself." It is the aid we give to the child so that the child might develop his or her own potential. It is the aid we give to Life with a capital L. In Montessori terms, through the experience of Life itself, the child performs his or her tasks as a builder of the mature human being.

As previously mentioned in chapter 8, the phrase that synthesizes the Montessori method of education is, "Help me to do it by myself." Likewise, as catechists we attend to the silent plea of the child, "Help me to draw close to God by myself."

Chapter 10

The Four Phases of Development and Education

Now let us consider this diagram (shown below): the natural growth of the person, which is based on scientific and objective data.

We can imagine the top line as a building being constructed floor by floor. The construction of each floor depends on the completion and preparation of the floor that precedes it, and in turn, each floor is a foundation for the next one. Obviously, one cannot begin constructing a building with the second floor. It is necessary to start with the foundation if we want to construct a solid building that will last. With regard to religious formation, can we say that when we begin with the

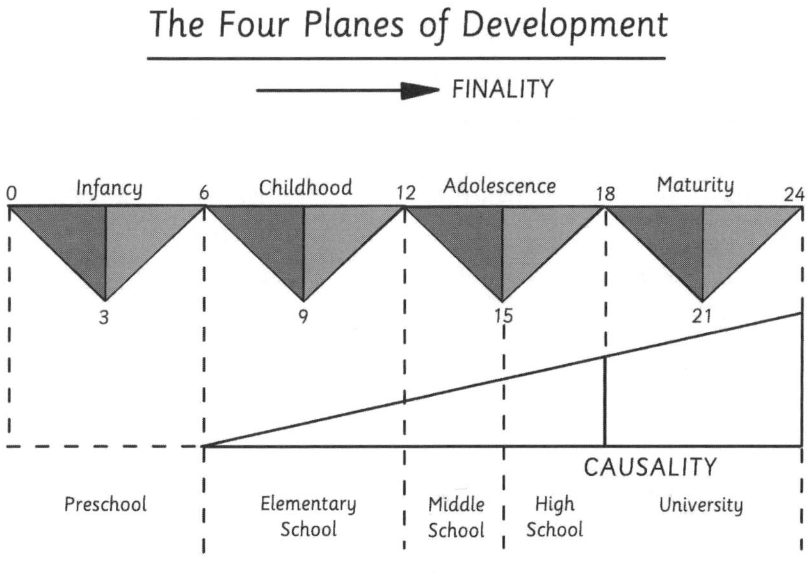

second floor—that is, after the age of six—we are constructing a solid building?

Let us now consider in detail the first two phases on the diagram—infancy and childhood. Our catechetical work unfolds in these two phases. Notice that the four phases, infancy, childhood, adolescence, and maturity, are differentiated by alternating screens of gray. The gray screens represent subphases that are characterized by intense, constructive work. These subphases are followed by more tranquil and less creative subphases during which the earlier, intense work is being consolidated. The choice using the triangle to represent this development is intentional—it is meant to point out that there is a period of greater intensity during every phase of the lifeline, which then decreases once a maximum is achieved.

Accordingly, the first triangle is divided into two sections, or subphases, corresponding to the periods from ages 0 to 3 and from 3 to 6. This first phase of development—infancy—is distinguished from all the others by the distinctive quality of the child's mind, which Montessori referred to as "the absorbent mind." The child is constantly absorbing knowledge, not by an intellectual or instructional route but as if by osmosis. A primary example of this is the way a young child learns language. The absorbent mind is most intensely at work during the first subphase, 0–3, but remains active in the second subphase as well. The adult cannot intervene directly in this work but can only offer peripheral assistance.[1]

Today, the nature of this phase of development and its importance for the future of humankind are much better known, as this phase has been carefully and scientifically observed by experts. Dr. Silvana Montanaro, an expert in child psychology as well as a seasoned Montessori practitioner and trainer, has focused particular attention on the first subphase of development. She reports her experiences and observations of the very young—0–3 years of age. She shares details of her work in preparing an environment, including specially trained personnel, to assist in infancy.[2] (The assistance offered is both for the infant/toddler and for the parents.)

1. Maria Montessori, *The Absorbent Mind* (Amsterdam: Montessori-Pierson Publishing, 2019), chapter 3: "The Periods of Growth."
2. Silvana Montanaro, *Understanding the Human Being: The Importance of the First Three Years of Life* (San Francisco: Nienhuis Montessori, 1991).

For the young child, the world is full of surprises and wonder. This is also the time of the greatest transformations in the child. Observing a child from birth to one year, we note the great differences from a child of three years who can talk, walk independently, and so on. Furthermore, in the phase from 0 to 6 years, the foundations are laid for all the psychic characteristics that will accompany the child throughout life and will constitute the child's personality.

Going on to the second phase, that of childhood, from 6 to 12 years of age, we find a relatively quiet, stable period of development. During this time the child assimilates all that was developed in the preceding phase. The child's body is also undergoing a process of consolidation. This phase is normally one of strength, health, and stability. The child cuts his or her second set of teeth, and the child's bones solidify.

If the child's natural strengths have not been hindered or suffocated in the preceding phase, this phase becomes one of serenity and poses no great difficulties of a psychic and educational nature. Traditionally, society has recognized competence on the part of the child in this phase of development when, usually at age 6, the child is considered qualified to begin formal studies.

Big changes can be noted in the third phase of development—adolescence. The glands are working to make the individual sexually mature. The body grows rapidly and seems out of proportion with its small chest and lungs that do not supply enough oxygen for the long body surface. This physical imbalance is mirrored in a sort of psychic imbalance often found in adolescents.

Indeed, the adolescent is emotionally volatile and somewhat inconstant: one moment he or she is full of enthusiasm and, in the next moment, is apathetic. Often during this phase of development, one experiences the thrill of a vocational "calling" or a vision of what one wants to become or accomplish in the world. The number of adolescent saints and martyrs attests to this fact. On the other hand, it can become the age of juvenile delinquency.

Also, adolescence is the phase when one becomes an individual member of society. Thus, it is a period of crisis that, once overcome, allows one to enter into the fullness of one's own energies and capabilities. Accordingly, as Montessori stressed, the adolescent should not be abandoned to find his or her own way. In fact, the adolescent is like the newborn who needs help in many ways. The adolescent is in a sort of birth process leading to a new form of life, and he or she needs our assistance just as much as the newborn does. If this assistance is not offered, the adolescent is at high risk for deviation and, even, for ruin.

The fourth phase of development, maturity, is, or should be, another phase of relative peace and stability. The physiological formation of the individual is completed with the cutting of the wisdom teeth. For many persons, it is the period of university studies, which really ought to be seen as a sort of "training ground" in which the person is formed to be open to others and clear about his or her own life choices. Tranquility and the capacity for absorption are characteristic of this phase. If the preceding period has been good, this phase will be a period in which the fruits of all the preceding phases will be harvested.

Although these four phases are distinct periods of growth and development, preceding and following one another, they are also interlaced and form a unity in the impulses that compel human beings toward the goal to which they are attracted. Human beings naturally aspire to something greater than themselves. Thus, education should aid their formation so that they may not only reach for but also find ever higher ideals.

The four phases, with their psychosomatic characteristics as delineated by Maria Montessori, are confirmed and enriched today through the studies and experiences of experts in various parts of the world. From this outline of the natural educational plan, founded on the science of education and its application, we may easily understand the expression "The child is father of the man."[3]

---

3. A frequent Montessori reference to William Wordsworth's poem "My Heart Leaps Up."

Chapter 11

The Sensitive Periods

The following discussion of sensitive periods is not intended to be a complete and exhaustive study of child psychology. Rather, it deals with a fundamental topic in Maria Montessori's thought, which can help us to know the child, who is the basis of Montessori's discovery and, thus, the basis of all her work in education.

In Montessori's first experiment with religious education in Barcelona, she rediscovered something she had already observed in the Children's House: even before culture and doctrine are taught, there already exists a vital relationship between the soul of the child and God. In her book *The Discovery of the Child,* Montessori suggested that the experience of religious education must open necessary relationships between the two branches of education: that which deals with the nature of the child in relationship to the reality of the exterior world, and that which touches the child's nature in relationship to the reality of the supernatural life.[1]

A greater understanding of the needs of the child in the psychic sphere can aid us in understanding and respecting the needs of the child in the religious sphere. To know, at least to some degree, the true nature of the child means to help the child in ways that will allow him or her to develop as an integrated, or whole, person—one who is in right relationship with self, with God, and with others.

The formation of a person unfolds as a unified process in four phases of development. These four periods of growth are represented in our diagram (page 65) by triangular forms. As previously noted, the choice of such a figure is not by chance but is intentional. The left side of the triangle signifies an increased intensity of creativity. The vertex of the triangle represents the maximum achievement of this intensity.

1. Maria Montessori, *The Discovery of the Child*, The Montessori Series, vol. 2 (Amsterdam: Montessori-Pierson Publishing, reprinted 2020), chapter 22.

The right side of the triangle represents a gradual decrease in creative intensity, until it finally disappears. At this point, a succeeding phase appears with its own new wealth of creative intensity. These periods are present throughout the entire line of human development, manifesting themselves in different ways.

In the course of human development, one sensitivity is a preparation for the next sensitivity of the succeeding phase; furthermore, all these sensitivities are interconnected and interdependent for the purpose of constructing a unified person. These growth periods or triangles thus represent periods of particular, intense sensitivities. Psychologists speak of "critical points" in the programming of the child's life. Maria Montessori called these critical points "sensitive periods." She speaks of how "the study of the sensitive periods might be compared to an exploratory operation which enables us to see the functioning of the various organs that promote the growth of the child. They show us that a child's psychic development does not take place by chance, that it does not originate in external stimuli but is guided by transient sensibilities—that is, by temporary instincts intimately connected with the acquisition of specific traits."[2]

Thus, the sensitive periods guide the development and determine the conquests of a psychic order. They also determine the capacities that, once acquired, will remain with the person throughout life. For this reason, the adult must be careful to recognize the moment of the sensitive period, to respect it, and to assist it, for once this sensitivity has passed, the opportunity for a natural acquisition is forever lost.

The same achievements can occur at a later time in the child's life but with a great burdening of the will, not as a spontaneous fact. Montessori pointed to the fact that "the sensitive periods push the child to do, with extraordinary joy, an infinite number of things that are constructive for him." The environment assists and cultivates these "sensitive periods."[3]

Montessori further develops this point in saying that the sensitive periods "enable the child to choose from this complex environment what is suitable and necessary for his growth. They make the child

2. Maria Montessori, *The Secret of Childhood*, The Montessori Series, vol. 22 (Amsterdam: Montessori-Pierson Publishing, reprinted 2017), 30.

3. Montessori, *The Secret of Childhood*, chapter 7.

sensitive to some things but leave him indifferent to others. When a particular sensitivity is aroused in a child, it is like a light that shines on some objects but not on others, making of them his whole world."[4]

The sensitive periods are a phenomenon of life, such as in the insect world, though of course with certain differences. This was discovered by the Dutch botanist Hugo de Vries (1848–1935), who dedicated himself to experimental research in the field of genetics and to the physiology of the animal and vegetable world.

In observing the behavior of caterpillars of common butterflies, de Vries noted that, as soon as the caterpillar hatches, it has a particular sensitivity to light. This sensitivity compels the caterpillar to come out of the hole in the tree trunk where the mother caterpillar had deposited her eggs and to find the tender leaves necessary for nourishment.

Once it is grown, the caterpillar will lose its sensitivity to light. The caterpillar does not become blind to the light, but rather, indifferent to it. In this succeeding phase of metamorphosis of the insect, it also develops an incredible voracity for a different kind nourishment that prepares the caterpillar for the fasting period of the larva stage of its development.

As Montessori notes in *The Secret of Childhood*, "The Dutch scientist Hugo de Vries discovered the sensitive periods in animals, but it was we, in our schools, who discovered that they are also to be found in children and can be used in teaching."[5]

The sensitive periods that are most unknown to us are those that occur in the child between 0 and 3 years of age. Yet the sensitive periods of this stage of development are the most important ones. Indeed, they form the pillars on which the construction of the person rests.

There are numerous studies today on early childhood development and education. As noted previously, an excellent source for understanding more about the first three years of the child's life is Dr. Silvana Montanaro's book *Understanding the Human Being.*[6]

Montessori observed that the child in this first phase of development has a fervor, a sort of hidden frenzy, toward language. Who

4. Montessori, *The Secret of Childhood*, 30.
5. Montessori, *The Secret of Childhood*, 28.
6. Silvana Montanaro, *Understanding the Human Being: The Importance of the First Three Years of Life* (San Francisco: Nienhuis Montessori, 1991).

among us has not witnessed a little child straining with great physical intensity to catch the movement and sounds coming from an adult's mouth? It is through this strong and secret attraction, whose mechanism is still unknown to us, that the child is being prepared for the acquisition of language. For the moment, the very young child can only respond to our words with an expression of great delight; but at some later moment, without any direct teaching on our part, the child suddenly speaks.

Even if the whole family celebrates this event, we do not necessarily reflect on how extraordinary it is. At some level we simply take these accomplishments for granted, assuming they are matters of course in human development. But have we ever thought about how much force of will it takes for us as adults to learn a foreign language?

This first strong attraction loses its intensity, although the child does not lose interest in language altogether. Indeed, if the child has been helped by the adult environment, the attraction continues and evolves into a capacity for expressing his or her needs, desires, and feelings. In the sphere of religious education, we have noted that children from around three years of age show a great interest in solemn and lofty-sounding names, such as those given to the Messiah in Isaiah's prophecy: "Wonderful Counselor, Mighty God, Everlasting Father, Prince of Peace" (Isaiah 9:6, NRSVUE).

It has been noted that the sensitive periods of this first phase, from 0 to 3 years, are not all as visible and identifiable as the one for language. Yet we can see that the strong attraction the child has toward language extends to other things the child finds in his or her environment. Indeed, it is the attraction to the environment that will guide the child in succeeding stages of development.

Compelled by diverse interests, the child will seek to interact with and come to know his or her environment. In the earliest phase of development, this attraction leads the child to become oriented to his or her surroundings, to distinguish people and things, and to situate them according to their function and place. This same attraction to the environment compels the child to move progressively until he or she is able to walk independently. It will compel the child to want to touch things, to imitate what adults do, and to choose the things that most correspond to the child's interests in order to know them both sensorially and intellectually.

Attraction to the environment will later put the older child in touch with the wider world, the world of his or her culture. It will compel him or her to explore the secrets of nature, the facts of human history, and the thoughts of human beings; it will inspire the child to form relationships and to experience "the other." The attraction to the environment is like a beacon of light that makes visible for the baby, the child, and the adult the things that most correspond to his or her developmental need.

If, at the beginning of its manifestation, the period of attraction to the environment has been respected in its phase of maximum intensity, then the child will enter actively into life; otherwise, the child will remain passive and dependent. Even if the child could change or improve, it would have to be done with very conscious and deliberate effort; it will not occur naturally or spontaneously.

The most important sensitive period in the first phase of development is that of order. It is also the most difficult one to recognize and interpret. Furthermore, it is obscured by the ambivalence that the word *order* generates in our adult minds. The sensitive period for order manifests itself during the first year of life and continues into the second year, with equal strength and intensity though with different internal motivations. It calls for loving, attentive observation on the part of the adult, so that it may lead the way to a harmonious relationship between the adult and the child.

Order does not have the same meaning for the child as for the adult, who insists upon it for the very practical reason that order allows for greater comfort in daily life and more efficiency in one's work. For the young child, order signifies the necessity of having fixed points of reference among the people and things that surround him or her. Finding familiar people and things in their same places gives the child a sense of security; and this security will form the basis of the harmonious construction of the person.

The full and harmonious development of the person requires an internal order, signifying that one has a clear awareness of self and of one's own place in his or her environment. After the age of three this developing internal order focuses more on intellectual pursuits and then on moral reasoning (after 6 years of age). We can observe the satisfaction that this kind of order brings in the pleasure a very young child (even just a few months old) shows when hearing the same song sung by the same person. Later, it will be a familiar story that the child delights in hearing told always with the same words. If we change the words, the child is sure to protest!

Around the age of two the child loves to put things back in their proper place and to take his or her usual seat at the table or in the car. When this need for order is not respected, it can provoke immediate and intense emotional reactions in the child, which adults often interpret as temper tantrums.[7]

If the familiar order is reestablished and, thus, the child's need is satisfied, everything returns to normal and the emotional eruption vanishes without a trace. Otherwise, it can become fixed in the child's behavior and, when the child is older, can generate major upsets or even character deviations that will require the adult's particular attention.

Montessori spoke of the educational process of "normalization," whereby the child learns to interact harmoniously with others in a community setting. This means that he or she can accept and comply with the norms or standards of behavior necessary for communal life (such as school life or family life). The more the child's deep needs are met, particularly in this first phase of development, the less likely intervention will be needed later in order for "normalization" to occur.

Besides those already indicated, there are other sensitive periods that can be identified in the period between birth and three years of age. For example, the one for sensorial development begins in this period, with the child's desire to put objects in the mouth and touch everything in order to know his or her environment. The sensitive period for movement manifests itself from the first days of life. If left free, the newborn moves. Already he or she is attracted to the environment, and this attraction that compels the baby to move is so strong that it will eventually lead to the baby's crawling, and then walking.

In the first phase of development, beginning even before birth and remaining particularly strong during the first three years of life, the

7. On this subject, we invite the reading of two particular episodes recorded by Montessori in her books *The Child in the Family* (pp. 8 and 9) and *The Secret of Childhood* (pp. 39–42).

need and capacity for relationship is paramount in the construction of the person. The newborn fixes his or her greatest attention on the human face, especially the face of the mother. Very early on, the baby recognizes and responds to the voice, the face, and the touch of the parent or primary caregiver. Interwoven in this need and capacity for relationship is the sensitive period for protection, which also deeply affects the formation of the person.

Although Montessori did not name or identify a specific religious sensitive period, she did observe and speak about a particular interior sensibility in young children, which she referred to as a "religious or spiritual sense." It is manifested in the awe and enjoyment of the children (from around 3 years of age, if not earlier) when presented the Christian Mystery, when engaging in the silence exercises, and when participating in simple rituals like carrying religious articles in a procession. In the chapter "Religious Education," Montessori summarizes her observations of the "religious sense" in children in this way: "[The children] show pleasing self-confidence, courage, a calm knowledge of things, above all, faith in God, the author and preserver of life."[8]

The children are so capable of distinguishing between natural and supernatural matters that their insight has given us the idea that there exists a period especially sensitive to religion. The age of childhood seems to be bound closely to God, as the development of the body is strictly dependent on the natural laws which are transforming it at that time."[9]

Montessori also identified sensitive periods in the second subphase of development—from 3 to 6 years of age (the age of the children in the Children's Houses)—when the child uses all the senses to distinguish, classify, generalize, and eventually to make abstractions about the objects in the environment. During this same period there is a sensitivity to reading and writing. In the Children's House one can readily observe the great interest and delight the child takes in learning these skills, unlike the struggle children can have if they are taught to read and write too late.

---

8. Maria Montessori, *The Discovery of the Child*, The Montessori Series, vol. 2 (Amsterdam: Montessori-Pierson Publishing, reprinted 2020), 320.
9. Montessori, *The Discovery of the Child*, 320.

In the succeeding phase of development, the period of the elementary school, there is a sensitive period for culture when the child discovers the relationship between the secrets of nature and human society. Also, during this period from age 6 to 9 there is a sensitive period for moral reasoning. The child of this age has a particular sensitivity toward and interest in distinguishing good from evil, as well as between right and wrong actions. If we try to engage the child in moral reasoning at an earlier age, when a natural interest in moral issues has not yet awakened in the child, we risk making him or her either overscrupulous or insensitive.

The importance of age-appropriateness in direct moral teaching is meaningfully illustrated in a story reported by Sofia Cavalletti.[10] She tells of a nursery schoolteacher who tried to tell young children the parable of the prodigal son. Toward the end of the parable, the prodigal son has wasted all his money and has been reduced to poverty and near starvation. He then leaves his menial job of tending pigs and returns to his father's house, where he is greeted with open arms. When the teacher finished recounting the parable, the children expressed the focus of their concern with the question, "What happened to those pigs?" The message of mercy and forgiveness seemingly escaped them. Because they were in a sensitive period for protection their focus was on the abandoned pigs! Only later, between 9 and 12 years of age, does a social sense fully awaken and take on greater significance in the child's life. Children of this age feel responsible for their actions toward other people. This is the time when young people particularly need good behavior models and, even more, a guide who can offer direction and enlightenment in their development of conscience.

Something similar to the sensitive periods occurs in a deeper part of the human psyche. Sofia Cavalletti talks about the existence of "vital exigencies" or deep, vital needs of the human person: "The child's psychological configuration is rooted at a deeper level than whatever the child may have lived, in the sense that there are vital exigencies that remain alive when they are gratified, but that are also present

10. Sofia Cavalletti, *The Religious Potential of the Child* (Chicago: Catechesis of the Good Shepherd Publications, 2020), 119.

almost like an unappeased hunger even when they do not find their satisfaction."[11]

She uses the term *constants* in reference to the common reactions of children to certain religious themes. These constants function as indicators or manifestations of the vital exigencies. Furthermore, the same basic reactions are observed in children of different social classes and diverse cultures. Children of a particular developmental phase tend to react in the same way to certain points of the Christian message.

Not only do the constants verify the existence of something like a religious sensitive period, they also indicate that the content of the message needs to vary according to the developmental stage of the child. In other words, the deep changing needs of the respective developmental period call for a different "face of God" to be presented. Accordingly, Cavalletti says, "For catechesis to be a living event for the child, the catechist should know the child's exigencies and the aspect of God that most corresponds to him or her."[12]

For the younger child, the "face of God" that is most gratifying is that of Jesus, the Good Shepherd. The parable of the Good Shepherd (found in John 10) contains a message of the totality and universality of God's love. The very completeness of this love finds a response in all human situations. Furthermore, the meaning of the parable continues to unfold as one grows:

- *The Shepherd calls the sheep by name.* This establishes a fundamental relationship between God and the individual. It is a relationship with a Person who responds to the deepest and most unexpressed needs of the individual.
- *The Shepherd takes care of the sheep, giving them everything they need.* His love protects and heals.
- *The Shepherd delights in being with his sheep.* When he finds the sheep that was lost, he "lays it on his shoulders and rejoices" and later, upon bringing it home, calls upon his friends and neighbors to celebrate the sheep's return together (Luke 15:3–6 NRSVUE).
- *The flock of the Good Shepherd is the community of faith, the Church,* into which we are welcomed at baptism.

11. Cavalletti, *The Religious Potential of the Child*, 136.
12. Cavalletti, *The Religious Potential of the Child*, 140.

- Beginning around 6 years of age, in the moral sensitive period, the child finds in the *parable of the found sheep a model of God's love which pardons and forgives.*
- At a still later age, the child focuses on the *Shepherd as the one who goes ahead and shows the way.* He, who "lays down his life for the sheep," models complete self-giving. Thus, for adolescents, the figure of the Shepherd is newly important in guiding their personal choices as well as their willing participation in the life of the community.
- The "one flock" that the Shepherd says will be formed someday represents the *final completeness of all created beings in God.*

There are other themes, lifted up through other presentations to the child, which also demonstrate the constants and religious sensitivities:

- Joy and a sense of security in response to the image of Christ as Light, as experienced through the sensorial character of the signs of light and darkness. This theme is lifted up through various presentations to the children during the year, but it is the celebration of the Liturgy of the Light at Easter when we see their fullest response.
- Wonder and delight in exploring the mystery of the kingdom of God. This is most evident when the child encounters the mustard seed (Matthew 13:31–32), so tiny but so empowered by the strength of God within that it grows into a tree. The child easily identifies and marvels over this same reality at work within himself or herself: the mystery of the kingdom of God as the mystery of life itself, a mystery of growth and transformation.

Moreover, as is evidenced in the parable of the seed of grain (Mark 4:26–29), this growth and transformation happens through a power that is not our own. We can see that in their response to the parable of the grain of wheat (John 12:24), the children also readily embrace the ultimate mystery of transformation: the mystery of death and resurrection.

Just as the sensitive periods guide the construction of the personality on a natural plane, these constants show us how the child's relationship with God is being built through a continually developing awareness of God. In the religious experience—that is, in the contact with the Person of God, there is gratification of an existential need, a deep satisfaction that seems to spill over and flow into the harmonious formation of the person.

Chapter 12

Freedom, Independence, and Discipline

We have already offered some practical suggestions as to how we can create an atmosphere of work and concentration in the atrium, while respecting the freedom of the child. Among other things, we have spoken about how to help the child gain independence, develop his or her capacity for concentration, and respect the work of others. Now we would like to go more deeply into the importance of freedom, both in the conquest of independence and in the overall formation of the child's person.

The value of freedom in the educational process is being recognized more and more. It is important to be clear about what Maria Montessori means when she speaks of the freedom of the child. The relationship between freedom and independence is primarily a philosophical problem and, as such, does not concern us. What is of particular interest to us, however, is the effect freedom and independence have on the formation of the person.[1]

Montessori wrote: "An educational method that shall have liberty as its basis must intervene to help the child to a conquest of these various obstacles. In other words, his training must be such as shall help him to diminish, in a rational manner, the social bonds which limit his activity. Little by little, as the child grows in such an atmosphere, his spontaneous manifestations will become clearer, with the clearness of truth, revealing his nature."[2]

Clearly, we are dealing with a freedom that is understood as liberation of the potentiality of the person and, therefore, as obedience

1. Maria Montessori, *The Discovery of the Child*, The Montessori Series, vol. 2 (Amsterdam: Montessori-Pierson Publishing, reprinted 2020), 72–88.
2. Montessori, *The Discovery of the Child*, chapter 4.

to a vital impulse that is presupposed to be toward the positive. This important capacity for freedom requires respect, and at the same time, it requires appropriate assistance so that freedom can be a conquest and not merely a free gift. Moreover, we could say that the real value of freedom lies in the fact that it is a conquest, a conquest involving response to and claim of what is good and right.

The art of the educator consists precisely in discerning when the child of a particular age or stage of development is or is not following this inner impulse toward truth and what is good. The good teacher or "directress," as Montessori termed the educator, understands and recognizes the difference between freedom and license, the negative manifestations of which are laziness, disorderly conduct, and so on. To respect the child's freedom is not to permit the child to do whatever he or she pleases, such as putting her feet on the table, shoving his companions around, and the like. When such negative behaviors occur, we intervene and correct.

As Montessori clarified, "Freedom has as its limitation the interests of the group and as its form that which we call teaching of manners: every manifestation which offends or harms others, or all that signifies unseemly or discourteous behavior, is to be prevented."[3]

Anna Maccheroni, one of Montessori's closest collaborators, told of how deeply upsetting it was to Montessori when those trained in her method failed to distinguish between freedom and license. In visiting schools following her method and in observing misbehavior being allowed in some misguided attempt to respect the child's freedom, she would go so far as to regret ever having developed the method.

The freedom of the child, understood as liberation, has to be respected at all times so that the child's potentialities might manifest themselves in different forms and in accordance with the characteristics of the child's developmental stage. For example, a newborn needs freedom of movement in order to achieve independence in walking; the confines of a tiny crib with high rails constitute a lack of freedom. The young child wants to be free in order to know the things of the environment that surround him or her. For this reason, in Montessori schools we provide children with various opportunities to attend to

3. Montessori, *The Discovery of the Child*, 87.

practical life tasks that help them to be independent in their environment. Gradually, as the child's capacity and need for contact with his or her culture grows, we give the child more and more options of freely chosen work. The work choices will continue to evolve, according to the spontaneous manifestations and potentialities of the child.

We have said that the conquest of freedom requires assistance, because the child left unaided, without the opportunity of work, would be lost, just as the newborn, without someone to provide nourishment, would die of hunger. We aid the freedom of the child with a prepared environment, suited to the spontaneous manifestations of the child, in which there can develop free, ordered work. The prepared environment makes possible the realization of a freedom that leads to independence. Then the extension and application of the freedom that is given to the child can grow and can become a true conquest based on self-discipline, not just a free gift.

In 1907, Maria Montessori's first experiment in the Children's House yielded a discovery of the true nature of the children and their capacities. In an environment carefully planned and constructed to consider the needs and manifestations of the children, Montessori freed the children from the restrictive norms of subjection, common to the educational methods of her time; she gave children the ability to move around, to choose work, and to express themselves. One must remember that in those days children were forced to remain seated the whole time they were in school; they were not allowed to speak or to move about without permission.

The phenomenon of spontaneous self-discipline, which was later observed in other cultural settings, could not have been ascertained in a different, more restricted environment. It was not a question of sporadic instances of self-discipline but of a spontaneous, natural phenomenon, and Montessori was convinced that there exists within the child an internal impulse that guides him or her toward order and independence.

If we adults impede the child from acting freely, we distance ourselves from the child and are no longer able to know his or her true needs. If we intervene and impose our will and judgements, and do for them what they need to do for themselves, then children cannot achieve true independence.

For us adults it is often very difficult to respect the liberty and independence of the child because we do not have sufficient faith in his or her capabilities or possibilities. We are impatient and are always ready to accomplish a task for the child ourselves. It is easier for us to do it ourselves rather than take the time to teach the child how to do it for himself or herself; yet this results in the child's becoming incapacitated and more dependent on us.

In the section "Independence," Maria Montessori writes: "A pedagogical action that is effective for the children must be one that helps them advance on their way to independence (understood in the manner of initiating them to those first forms of activity that enable them to be sufficient in themselves and not to lean on others because of their own inability). Helping them learn to walk without assistance, to run, to go up and down stairs, to pick up fallen objects, to dress and undress themselves, to wash themselves, to speak in order to clearly express their own needs and their own feelings, to search with efforts to arrive at the satisfaction of their desires—this is education to independence."[4]

The independent child, unhindered by interference, limitations, or lack of opportunity, has proven that he or she follows an interior impulse toward acquiring and developing capabilities; this may come as a surprise to those who observe the child. To be independent means to be free and not to be dependent on others, because I find that I am capable of doing what I need to do. So do I acquire confidence in myself, in discovering my own capabilities. So, too, does a person become secure in himself or herself, a strong "I" who will know how to choose the good and reject the evil, a person who will know how to be oneself.

The example of the paralytic and the prince, neither of whom can take off his own shoes—one because of a physical disability and the other because of rules of social formality—reveals that both are in the same situation, because both the prince and the paralytic are dependent on someone else. A person who is served (or attended by servants) instead of merely being assisted is, to some degree, robbed of his or her independence.[5] Today, this kind of service is very rare, and yet we still

4. Montessori, *The Discovery of the Child*, 57, 58.
5. Montessori, *The Discovery of the Child*, 62.

do not have a clear understanding of independence. Even though it has become easier for us to conceive of and respect the notion of the independence of others, we still readily become servile and often fail to see that this impedes the other person's independence. The one who serves and the one who is being served are then independent.

An education to independence also necessarily involves the conquest of a capacity for self-discipline. When we educators, teachers, or catechists speak of discipline we are usually referring to the capacity of a child or young person to behave in an orderly way and to comply with what is being asked of him or her. We immediately pose the question of which methods we should apply in order to obtain this result. But there are different kinds of discipline that we need to be able to distinguish according to the age or developmental stage of the child.

On discipline, Montessori points out: "There is a lack of discipline in the very small child who is still incapable of disciplined acts, because he has not achieved coordination of movements (his neuromuscular system has not yet matured). This child is not only to be respected but is to be helped indirectly, through intelligent activity: objects to gather together, to manipulate, to carry; learning to eat, and so forth. He repeats the same gestures, tries, and tries again until he succeeds in obtaining his goal; in this way he acquires a discipline of actions which will render him independent in doing things. The entire prepared environment helps him to do and makes him independent. This quality of discipline is not the result of an external will which comes from an adult who wants the child orderly and quiet. It is a response to an interior order, like an exercise of discipline."[6]

There is another type of discipline that we might refer to as "traditional"; it constitutes the problem with which we adults are preoccupied. We adults tend to think that discipline is obtained through the application of common corrective techniques, through persuasive speeches, scolding, and commands. Although, in certain cases with older children, this type of discipline might be useful or even necessary and may seem to be effective for a time, it loses its power and necessity as soon as the child becomes engaged in a freely chosen work. The act of choosing and becoming absorbed in a work makes way for a spontaneous

6. Montessori, *The Discovery of the Child*, chapter 24.

kind of discipline, springing from an internal source, and then coming to take direction from and be obedient to the will. This is the sort of discipline that Maria Montessori observed in children, a discipline that is spontaneous and natural.

From such a perspective, we can then see in the child a transformation that often astonishes us and that is reflected in the children as a group. We witness the phenomenon of concentration and constancy in work. The child shows himself or herself to be capable of self-discipline because this is an impulse that comes from the depths of the child's being and is directed toward self-confidence, independence, and the expansion of the common well-being of the group as a whole.

Order and discipline are rightly to be expected, not only out of respect for the needs and norms of the community, but also out of respect for the order and discipline that are called for from within the child. The child is capable of balancing harmoniously the needs of the community with his or her own needs, which contributes to the child's mental order.

If the premise of freedom is rightly understood, if the teacher in the Children's House knows how to limit her intervention in the work of the child and how to exercise her authority sparingly, then, after a period of adaptation and normalization, the children will achieve a spontaneous discipline. Anyone who visits well-run Montessori schools is struck by the various individual activities going on. Some children are working on the floor, others at little tables, with such concentration and a kind of silence that is broken only by the bustle of the work itself, like a swarming beehive. Furthermore, the organization of work could serve as a model for adults.

It is important to note that this atmosphere of work and concentration is not dependent on the presence of the teacher or supervising adult. In fact, once the children are engaged in their work, they barely recognize the presence of the adult! This is indicative of a level of order or organization that is not like an external order or an order imposed on the child from outside; rather, it corresponds to the internal order that exists within each child.

In the atrium, the concentration that springs from discipline and work leads to meditation and prayer. This is the goal toward which the child strives in order to encounter God. It is very important that we assist the child in meeting this goal so that he or she may realize the freedom of the children of God as described by St. Paul in the Bible: "The creation itself will be set free from its enslavement to decay and will obtain the freedom of the glory of the children of God" (Romans 8:21, NRSVUE).

Chapter 13

The Significance of Work

We could speak extensively on the theme of work. Psychology and sociology furnish us with a vast literature on the subject; all sectors of society are always interested in it. Here, we must limit ourselves to the consideration of just a few points that are of greatest interest to us.

From the beginning of the human species an intimate bond has been established between humanity and the environment, a bond that has been formed through work; for it is only through work, through using our intelligence and our other precious instruments such as our hands, that human beings have been able to take charge of our environment and transform it, and adapt the environment to ourselves.

The stimulus that has compelled and continues to compel human beings to work is that of survival, the satisfaction of vital needs, and the social bond. But work is also a response to a spontaneous and profound aspiration that is particular to human nature. The progress of civilization and culture is linked to our capacity for work—either as individuals or as members of a group—from which the whole of society benefits. The multiple forms and applications of work, its significance, and its role in society have changed throughout the centuries; however, work remains one of the principal manifestations of human behavior, a kind of instinct that is characteristic to the human species.

When we refer to the activities that the children carry out in the atrium, not just those that pertain to the liturgical celebrations and the Christian Proclamation but also the complementary activities, such as use of the catechetical materials, practical life tasks, art, handwork (see chapters 3 and 4), and so on, we speak of work and not of play.

Modern psychology defines play as a productive activity, not a mere pastime or diversion; it is seen as the best of activities, aimed toward the full realization of the individual. Hence, the fundamental importance of play has been clearly recognized. Play is a spontaneous activity, motivated by bio-psychic needs for development, and necessary for the construction of the psychic structures of the person. Therefore, the subject of play is a serious matter, but it is not the focus of our concern in these pages. We say that the children in the atrium work.

From her earliest experiences with children, Maria Montessori observed how readily they would abandon their familiar games and toys when offered the opportunity to engage in tasks with a useful and productive goal, such as setting a table, polishing one's shoes, dusting, washing, and the like. Each of the tasks involved the use of sensorial, culturally appropriate material, with the overall quality of authenticity (actual tools or working objects in miniature, not toys).

The questions of greatest interest to us that behavioral psychologists are also asking are: What internal stimulus motivates one to work? Why is one capable of work? How does this capability develop and progress? These questions interested Montessori and were at the forefront of her work with and discovery of the child. With the concept of "sensitive periods," which are the base of the psychic construction of the developing being, it is important to focus specifically on the sensitive period we have referred to as "attraction to the environment." It was on this element that Maria Montessori founded her "theory of work" with regard to the child.

As we have noted, beginning with her earliest experiences with children, she spoke of the child's activities in the Children's House as work rather than as play. She noted that an intimate bond forms between the child and the environment. Montessori observes, "So strong is this bond, from birth onwards, that it could be compared to the nervous reflex of muscles, constituted by the correspondence between sensation and motor reaction."[1]

Development and growth lead to an ever closer and more extensive relationship with the environment. The sensitive period of "attraction to the environment" is the sign of this bond, which will be permanently manifested in work.

If this interior sensitivity, the "attraction to the environment," is respected, it serves as a guide to the child, not only enabling the child

1. Maria Montessori, *The Absorbent Mind*, The Montessori Series, vol. 1 (Amsterdam: Montessori Pierson-Publishing, reprinted 2017), chapter 13.

to examine the environment but also to take possession of the things he or she needs within that environment, such as language. As this occurs, it will no longer be a matter of the child simply enjoying auditory and visual sensations; rather, the child will be compelled by the need to hear things and to touch things, as if the things around him or her were magnets, drawing the child to them. It is this very need that gives the child the capacity to penetrate the secrets of things around him or her, to know these things, and to love them. The child must find satisfaction for this "love"—an attraction so strong that it must be concretized. This happens in an activity, in a work.

As we begin to observe a little child and to accompany him or her with our mind, our heart, and our eyes, as we become attentive to the child's development and conquests, we become aware that already there already exists from birth an internal guide that compels the child to movement and leads him or her to activity and, from there, to contact with the environment. A first contact is established through the child's hand. In the words of Montessori, "The hand is that organ, fine and complicated in its structure, which permits intelligence not only to manifest itself, but to enter into special relationship with the environment. One can say that man takes possession of the environment with his hand and, guided by intelligence, transforms it, and thus completes his mission in the picture of the universe."[2]

If the hand has been the instrument of the development of humanity, then education or psycho-pedagogy ought to take it more into consideration, because we now know that the human person is constructed through the work of his or her hands. The hand and language are the instruments of intelligence. Accordingly, the Montessori method considers the work of the hands in all four stages of development. Naturally, the things the hands reach for, the ways the hands manipulate those things, and the abilities that are manifested through the hands, change as the needs of the child moving through the different developmental stages change. Montessori affirmed that the child's intelligence, which has reached a certain level with limited use of the hands, can reach a much higher level through manual activity and that the child who works with his or her hands has a stronger character.

2. Maria Montessori, *The Secret of Childhood*, The Montessori Series, vol. 22 (Amsterdam: Montessori-Pierson Publishing, reprinted 2017), 67.

Chapter 14

The Relationship between the Child's Work and Cosmic Work

The relationship the child has with his or her environment is of a particular character and differs from that which adults normally experience. It generates in the child an impassioned kind of work, the kind characterized by focused intensity that is often seen in scientists, explorers, and artists. When this same phenomenon occurs in adults, then their work is no longer heavy, boring, and exhausting, because it corresponds to the internal needs of the person.

Montessori observed: "When this happens, work becomes fascinating and irresistible and raises a man above his diverted self. He becomes possessed of an extraordinary power and experiences again that natural instinct that enables him to express his own individuality. This instinct is like a powerful stream that gushes forth from the earth and provides refreshment for humankind."[1]

It is this kind or quality of work that carries forward the development of humanity. As always, the world of nature can assist us in penetrating human phenomenon. The spontaneous, unconscious urge that compels the child to work is similar to those instincts that nature has placed in all living creatures, both in the animal and the plant kingdoms, which do their parts in preserving the earth. Obviously, animals do not work consciously in the same sense that humans do. They obey the instincts that nature has "programmed" within them; they obey these instincts without realizing they are doing so; and furthermore,

1. Maria Montessori, *The Secret of Childhood*, The Montessori Series, vol. 22 (Amsterdam: Montessori-Pierson Publishing, reprinted 2017), 166.

they "work" with a fidelity that reminds us of the small child who repeats and repeats his or her work with an intense exactness, dictated evidently from within.

If we explore in depth the work of many animals and insects, we see prodigious things; the work of God's creation unfolds before our eyes, and its reproduction, besides preserving the species, demonstrates another mysterious fact that has long been overlooked. All living creatures carry out specific tasks directed at their own survival: they nourish themselves, protect themselves, reproduce, and so on. But they also have another task, one whose scope reaches far beyond that of mere survival. They carry out a sort of "universal mission" given by nature, a mission that has to do with the interdependence of all living creatures.

Consider the example of bees, which labor to suck more nectar than they actually need for their own nourishment. In their frenzy to drink the nectar, they plunge deep into the corolla of the flower, into the innermost parts, right down to the ovary. Having filled themselves with pollen; they unwittingly transport it to other flowers and fertilize them. They are attending to their silent, unconscious work, and, in so doing, they are not only being nourished themselves, they are also ensuring the survival of certain plants.

These plants nourish us, heal us, and delight us. What's more, their work of respiration, in which they absorb carbon dioxide and release oxygen, provides us and all other animals with the air we need to breathe. Yet the plants live and do their work in part because of the bees doing their silent work as nature has commanded. This unconscious, faithfully executed, "cosmic work" is part of a universal, unconscious obedience, which for centuries has been harmonizing and uniting all living beings, even without their conscious recognition that it is so.

From its earliest manifestations, the work of the child participates spontaneously in this universal obedience. With certain differences, of course, the child is under the same direction as the cosmic work happening in nature. Furthermore, if a child was not born with this impassioned push toward the environment, this "love" that brings its vital force upon the earth, then, as Montessori once said, all would be lost.

The work of the adult is often so exhausting, burdensome, and different from the "impassioned" work of the child, that we can find it hard to believe that at the foundation of human life there can be another attitude toward work. Maria Montessori wondered whether our social concept of work as a tiring necessity is a later development of what happens in children, or a deviation.

On the difference between the work of the child and the work of the adult in *The Secret of Childhood* (chapter 27), Montessori said: "Both child and adult carry on an immediate, conscious, and voluntary action upon their environment that may be regarded as work in the proper sense of the term. But here the comparison ends since they each have a different goal to achieve which is not directly known and willed."[2] Montessori asserted that there are two essential types of work: that of the child and that of the adult, both of which are necessary for the life of humanity.

In order to lift up the preciousness of the child's work, Montessori compared the thread produced by the silkworm, from which fine, beautiful fabric is made, to the spider web that human beings are quick to destroy. The silk is the product of the child's being, while the spider web is the product of the adult. What interests us is the silk, the work of the child; thus, we want to observe the child and to learn how we can assist the child in his or her work.

Why is the child so active? Why does the child work? Because he or she is responding to an interior stimulus. Initially unconscious, it is a stimulus to do what he or she sees being done in the surrounding environment. Thus, to a degree, the stimulus is an inner push to conform oneself to the behavior models of the adults nearby, in harmony with the environment itself. Yet there is much more to this stimulus: otherwise, it would be a simple matter of imitation. The child has an inner drive to work because it is through work that the child builds his or her very self, while using and developing his or her primary instruments: hand and intelligence. The child works, not so much in order to learn as to become. This happens through repetition of the focused movement or activity. Therefore, the child is compelled to work by two stimuli: (1) an unconscious drive to interact with the environment that

2. Montessori, *The Secret of Childhood*, 171.

surrounds the child; and (2) a drive in the child to construct his or her own instruments. Gradually, as the work of the child becomes more conscious, it also becomes more explicit and is extended to the service of self and of others, which is the work of the adult. After the age of six, the child no longer does the repetitious kind of work that the younger child so needs to do (often repeating many times in succession even a single gesture, such as unscrewing a jar lid or opening a door).

Even though it is very important, the environmental factor in development is still secondary to the phenomenon of life itself. The environment can modify, assist, or even destroy the being, but it can never create the being. Accordingly, Montessori has said in *The Discovery of the Child*, "The origins of the development of the being are interior. The child does not grow because he breathes, nourishes himself, and lives in favorable climatic conditions. In fact, the adult who nourishes himself, breathes, and lives in favorable climatic conditions no longer grows (physiologically, that is). Puberty does not come because the child breathed, nourished himself, and stayed in a favorable climate, but because that physiological phenomenon has arrived. The environment may be more favorable or less favorable, but life continues to unfold and proceeds according to its natural laws within established boundaries."[3]

Today, environments specifically designed for children are more visible and widespread than they once were. Today's educational environments feature appropriate buildings and architectural designs and furnishings that are attractive and proportionate. (Even they are also sometimes too refined). Yet these factors alone would not be sufficient for the child's education if the environment were not intelligently prepared and predisposed to the work of the child.

When children have the possibility of a freely chosen work that allows them the opportunity to explore and discover things in detail and the secrets they hold, the children are drawn to the educational environment as the bee is drawn to the flower. Then the force of spontaneous work is manifested as a spontaneous response.

The child carries out this form of work according to his or her own rhythm. Unlike the adult, the child is not interested in utilizing

3. Maria Montessori, *The Discovery of the Child*, The Montessori Series, vol. 2 (Amsterdam: Montessori-Pierson Publishing, reprinted 2020), 62.

his or her energies for maximum results. High efficiency is not an issue for the child. Rather, the child works more for the pleasure of the work itself. He or she works largely without the need of praise or recognition and in an orderly way, often refusing the help of the adult. Indeed, the child will often say, "I want to do it myself." This quality of work and its development forms the base of healthy psychic life and paves the way for human solidarity.

Above all, our task is that of

- removing obstacles between the child and the environment,
- carefully observing the different manifestations of the child's work,
- adjusting ourselves to the child's rhythm of work, and
- proposing appropriate and intelligent projects and activities so that these delicate and powerful forces at work within the child will not be extinguished or misused but, instead, can be fully realized.

As we have noted, with our inappropriate interventions, impeding all kinds of work, we can derail the work of the child, the negative "fruits" of which can be disorderly conduct, outbursts of temper, apathy, and indifference. Instead, when the child is deeply touched by a work that interests him or her, he or she becomes intensely focused and peacefully engaged, and the work brings the child back to "normalcy" (or the state of being in harmony with self and environment).

In other words, when the child is engaged in a freely chosen work, we see a different child, one who is ordered, interested in things, active, and manifesting the phenomenon Montessori referred to as "normalization" (see chapter 11.) Montessori observed this phenomenon in children of all races and cultures, because universally, children are capable of finding the "norm," that law that guides their growth. Normalization is a response to the inner laws that God has placed at the base of Life. Moreover, work becomes a kind of reorganizer of the personality. Not only does work assist the building of the person, it can also be a critical means of rebuilding and reordering the person through reconnecting him or her with those inner laws. We have witnessed this phenomenon of normalization often in our atriums.

If we succeed in removing obstacles and in both providing for and respecting the work of the child, then great things will happen:

- The child will develop as nature intends.
- We will get to see how the human being is formed, the human being who is made "in the image of God" and according to God's desire.
- Work will become an instrument of normalization or wholeness, both in oneself and in one's relationship to the group.
- Work will become joyful for the child, and, once that occurs; we can offer the assistance the child needs.

Chapter 15

Helping the Child to Pray

If we want to assist the child in his or her religious experience, an important area to which we must attend is that of prayer. Prayer is, first of all, listening to God. It is the particular key that opens up the mystery of God's relationship with God's creature. It is a key that not only belongs to God, but that is also given to all God's creatures regardless of denomination, class, or race, one that is offered in every moment, place, and circumstance. As Christians we pray through the mediation of Jesus Christ. Our prayer is both a preparation and a vehicle for arriving at the greatest prayer of thanksgiving: the Eucharist.

Prayer is initiation to the mystery of God and is, itself, mystery. It is a means of knowing God: it is a means of God's self-revelation to us, and it is an instrument of our personal response to God. The Good Shepherd "calls his own sheep by name." This means that, as catechists, we cannot presume to teach prayer. Rather, our task is that of creating the conditions for silence and reverence that will help the child to focus on and listen to God. We do this, first of all, by preparing an environment with a prayerful atmosphere.

The Nature of the Child's Prayer

Each of us who has experienced the child praying knows how capable he or she is of spontaneous prayer, and how different that prayer is from that of the adult, both in form and content. The child's prayer has a special quality of silence and contemplation. For example, even a 1-year-old might enter into a long, contemplative silence when experiencing a sunset or the flight of a bird, and this can be considered prayer. One story goes of an old, humble man, who was sitting in the last pew of an empty church and seemed to be waiting for someone. When he was asked "What are you waiting for?" the old man just gazed at the tabernacle and answered, "I look at him, and he looks at me." The prayer of the child is of this same quality of spontaneity and authenticity, and it is these very qualities that form the base and the motivation of every initiation to prayer.

The child's prayer can be very brief, with single words such as "Jesus," "Goodness," "Light," or "Amen," then often followed by a long silence. After many years of observation of young children in the atrium, we have realized that the spontaneous prayer of the younger child is exclusively a prayer of praise and thanksgiving, rather than a prayer of petition. Thus, we hear younger children say: "Thank you for the light!" "Thank you for everything!" "Thank you because I am one of your sheep!" "Jesus is wonderful!" "My body is happy!"

Certainly, then, we must respect and encourage the spontaneous prayer of the child; however, we must also help them with more formal or structured prayer. We do this in order to enrich their personal prayer language, as well as to aid their participation in the liturgy of the Church. We want to help them find a balance between spontaneous and formal prayer, which can support and nourish them throughout their lives.

The Prayer Corner

Within the atrium we designate a space set apart from the rest of the work environment to be the prayer corner. In this space there will be a low table on a lovely rug that helps to define the space as special. The prayer table will be prepared by the children with particular articles: a colored cloth corresponding to the current liturgical season, a beautifully bound Bible, candles, and a sacred image (such as a statue of the Good Shepherd or the Madonna and Child, or an icon). Often there will be a vase of flowers, prepared by the children and placed on the table. Also, there is a kneeler or cushion to invite individual use of the prayer corner at times other than communal prayer sessions.

The catechist gathers the children in the prayer corner and invites them into silence. The catechist then darkens the room and lights the candles. There follows the recitation or singing of a psalm phrase and intervals of silence. The catechist should be positioned beside or behind the children, particularly if playing a musical instrument, and never in front of them so as not to distract their attention and concentration.

Prayer table with a kneeler

The length of the prayer time will be determined by the children and will often consist of long periods of silence, which are, themselves, authentic prayer. We may conclude the prayer session by inviting the children's verbal responses. The catechist must have great respect and patience in soliciting the spontaneous responses of the children.

All of this need not seem too formal because, particularly in the beginning, it is necessary to provide an exterior, structured form for prayer or, we might say, to create a kind of ritual for prayer. Obviously, this does not preclude the importance of other times of spontaneous prayer in the atrium, such as: when the children listen to the Word being proclaimed, or are working, or singing, or "listening" to the silence. However, the children love ritual; it seems to touch a deep need within them. The repetition of something they know and love gives them a sense of security. All who work with children, as catechists or as parents, have experienced the joy and the peace of children of all ages after a time of prayer. A ritual of prayer similar to what we do in the atrium. can also be done in the home.

Elements of Prayer

There are three important elements that aid prayer indirectly:

- silence,
- controlled movement, and
- language.

Each of these elements needs to be attended to separately with the children; various presentations and exercises in the atrium cultivate each of these elements.

Silence

It is difficult to find natural conditions of silence today. Life in a city, whether large or small, is filled with so many noises, up to the limits of human tolerance and even causing physical and psychological disturbance. Noise is one of the most serious pollutants on our planet. Even the quiet of the countryside, once a sanctuary of silence, is disrupted by the noise of farm machinery, passing cars, and airplanes overhead. The frequent use of tech devices while working or being engaged in other activities seems yet another indication that people do not want to be alone with themselves.

Our environment does not help us as it used to, and the extraordinary and inconceivable richness of silence easily escapes us. Today people are often involved in yoga and other relaxation techniques, if only for the physical and psychological benefits of silence and stillness. Monks and nuns, particularly those in contemplative orders, have for centuries been practicing and teaching silence as essential to prayer. Indeed, all God's teachings on prayer in the Bible point to the importance of silence and recollection.

God's self-revelation comes to us in silence. Jesus, himself, would go away from the crowd in order to communicate with his Father and gain strength from being close to God in silence. Jesus offers us some practical advice on prayer in saying: "Whenever you pray, go into your room and shut the door and pray to your Father who is in secret," (Matthew 6:6, NRSVUE). He tells us that, in order to find the interior silence necessary for prayer, we need to remove ourselves from all noise and activities that might disturb us.

Stillness and silence foster reflection and the capacity to listen to the Other, to receive God's presence in our whole being. According to God's teachings, an emptying of self is what God desires, an emptying of self that will allow God to fill us with the gift of God's own self.

We want to help the children become aware of the value of silence as a necessary means of listening and responding to God. With this purpose in mind, we go to the lesson of silence, as devised by Maria

Montessori. It is a fundamental, collective exercise that is also part of other movement lessons, such as "walking on the line" and "practical life."

These collective lessons and all the other individual activities that take place in the Children's House foster concentration, controlled movement, and self-discipline. But it is the lesson of silence that most helps the child to become aware of and to master his or her own actions.

We are not speaking of the silence that is sometimes demanded by a teacher in trying to restore order to a noisy classroom. This kind of silence is of very little value to anyone but the teacher. We could say that it is "an empty silence." The silence we want to establish is the one Maria Montessori describes as rising from stillness, or "immobility"; it is a silence that serves the child—it has substance, and it brings interior order. The children show us time and again how much they love this exercise of silence. Montessori tells of more than one incident when the children would become silent and still after the teacher had written only the first letter of the word *silence* on the blackboard. The lesson of silence, or silence game, is done in the following way:

- The catechist invites the children to find a comfortable position and calls their attention to her own stillness and silence. She calls the children to try and imitate her. (It's not easy!)
- Next, the catechist whispers a few brief suggestions to the children to help them become aware of their own bodies. Together we check to see that our feet, our legs, arms, and hands are still.
- We pay attention to our breathing to see that it, too, is quiet.
- When all are relatively silent, the catechist might invite the children to become aware of sounds around them: perhaps the sound of birds (or traffic) outside, the sound of water dripping, movement, or voices in the hallway, and so on. The catechist might also invite the children to close their eyes and listen for the sound she will make, such as ringing a small bell. Sometimes, when the silence is complete, and the children have had an opportunity to enjoy the silence for some time, the catechist can suggest in a low, solemn voice a psalm verse or a song.
- The silence exercise is concluded by the catechist going just outside the room and whispering each child's name. The child who is called gets up and moves as silently as possible to where the catechist is, while the other children wait with amazing patience and great anticipation for their names to be called.

Speaking of the silence exercise, Montessori said that the self-control the children managed to achieve gave them great joy, but their greater joy was in hearing something new and special in the silence. In *The Discovery of the Child*, she writes: "It was then that I learned that within the mind of the child dwells its own reward amid its own spiritual pleasures. After such exercises it seemed to me that their love was greater; they certainly became more obedient, sweeter, and gentler."[1] She goes on to say, "It is in silence and when movements are ordered that the inner sensitivity that is called 'religious sense' or 'spiritual sense' can be developed."[2]

Silence puts the child in touch with himself or herself, first, through awareness of one's body and the simple attention to one's own breathing. Doing the silence exercises also helps the child feel connected to the others in the group through the common effort of achieving the silence. Further, it sensitizes the child to the surrounding environment: in the silence we suddenly can hear the water running in the fountain, the ticking of the clock, the sound of the birds just outside the window. The experience of silence heightens the child's awareness of self, others, and the environment. It fosters a state of inner peace and thus, also, a greater capacity for listening to God.

All of Montessori pedagogy, if properly interpreted and applied, prepares within the child a fertile ground for prayer. However, the exercise of silence is of particular importance in nurturing the child's capacity for prayer. It serves as a point of departure and predisposes the child to prayer.

Silence needs to become a habit of being, and prayer, understood as dialogue, requires silence. It is in the silence that God speaks to us. It is in the silence that we can best listen and respond to God. If silence is an essential element in the Children's House, it is even more important in the atrium. We can even go so far as to say that without silence there is no prayer.

---

1. Maria Montessori, *The Discovery of the Child*, The Montessori Series, vol. 2 (Amsterdam: Montessori-Pierson Publishing, reprinted 2020), 150–151.
2. Montessori, *The Discovery of the Child*, 319.

Controlled Movement

Along with the exercise of silence, another indirect aid in developing the child's capacity for prayer regards movement. We seek to help the child learn to manage his or her own body, to control one's own movements. As we have said in the earlier chapter, "Welcoming the Children," lessons in controlled movement are given from the beginning of the atrium year. They help the children to know their environment and function successfully within it.

Some of the initial lessons in controlled movement include how to carry a chair, how to sit, how to carry an object or material, and so on. These exercises also help the child know himself or herself, as well as to form a group. It is up to us, as catechists, to make these exercises interesting and enjoyable.

All of these exercises can be seen as a preparation for the controlled movements, or gestures, which are part of our prayer language, such as genuflection, the sign of the cross, carrying sacred objects in processions, and so on. The hands, for instance, speak their own prayer language. The palms may be brought together (a gesture that can be found also in Eastern religions); or the hands and arms might be extended, as can be seen in early Christian art. The sign of the cross is, itself, an expression of one's relationship to God and offers its own opportunity for reflection.

These gestures are meant to be an outward expression of an interior disposition, both of which can lead to prayer. Thus, helping the child do these gestures is a further aid to their prayer. They are able to understand the meaning of the gestures and can readily and attentively achieve the various postures or controlled movements of the gestures.

The gestures are taught by imitation and simple explanation of their religious significance. The catechist first does the gesture slowly and silently in front of the child. The catechist might then position himself or herself beside the children and help them repeat the gesture. If a prayer is meant to accompany the gesture (for example, "In the name of the Father, and of the Son, and of the Holy Spirit."), it will be introduced at a later moment so as not to confuse the two languages of word and gesture.

Language

Keeping in mind that gestures are themselves a kind of language, we now address the other language of prayer: the way we express ourselves in words. Both the exercises of silence and of controlled movement enhance one's capacity to hear God's Word and to make it his or her own. The words and phrases from the Scriptures are also an essential ingredient in nurturing prayer language. The psalms, in particular, can help us express our feelings when our own words may be lacking. One's personal prayer can be greatly enriched by repeating words prayed over the centuries by others who have spoken with God (such as the prayer of David, the shepherd, Psalm 23).

There is a very wide choice of short psalm passages. The catechist selects some that lift up images for God and correspond to the younger child's most natural form of prayer: praise and thanksgiving. These might include: "The Lord God is a sun and shield" (Psalm 84:11, NRSVUE), "The Lord is king! Let the earth rejoice" (Psalm 97:1, NRSVUE), and "The Lord is God, and he has given us light" (Psalm 118:27, NRSVUE).

Other psalm passages are selected that focus on the two principal feasts, Christmas and Easter, and their respective times of preparation, Advent and Lent. For instance, in the Easter season, when we celebrate the Liturgy of the Light with the children, we might add to our collection of psalm phrases: "The Lord is my light and my salvation" (Psalm 27:1, NRSVUE).

The language of Sacred Scripture strikes the religious sensitivity of the child. In times of communal prayer, the children love to repeat the names of the Lord found in Isaiah's prophecy (Isaiah 9:6, NRSVUE): "Wonderful Counselor, Mighty God, Everlasting Father, Prince of Peace" or those names spoken by the angel at the annunciation: "Son of the Most High" and "Son of God." In her book *Spontaneous Activity in Education*, Maria Montessori talks about how the children are passionate lovers of words and how they (particularly the younger children) are in a sensitive period for language, manifested by a keen interest in words.[3]

3. Maria Montessori, *Spontaneous Activity in Education*, The Montessori Series, vol 9 (Amsterdam: Montessori-Pierson Publishing, 2018), chapter 4.

A 5-year-old child who, each night before going to bed, dearly loved to listen to the whole chant of Hananiah, Mishael, and Azariah, the three youths in the burning furnace, praising God for the works of creation (Daniel 2:20ff.). This child would even ask for the chant to be repeated in Latin. Obviously, he could not understand the actual words, but through the cadence, or "music," of the language, he was able to perceive its religious nature.

All this heritage of vocabulary, which the child easily absorbs, is often reflected in their prayer. Furthermore, as children grow older, their familiarity with the brief passages seems to go on enriching their prayer, both in content and form.

It is helpful to provide the children with a collection of "prayer cards" that are written in large, beautiful lettering and are kept in the prayer corner. These will include some one-word prayers (such as "Alleluia," "Hosanna," "Amen"), some brief psalm phrases, and the prophecies of Advent. Also included in the collection are some short prayer samples found in the infancy narratives in the Gospels, such as Mary's words of highest praise in the Visitation account: "My soul proclaims the greatness of the Lord; my spirit rejoices in God my Savior." Or the angels' song of praise at the birth of the Lord: "Glory to God in the highest."

Prayers

The child might choose a prayer card to place on the prayer table as part of his or her personal prayer; the catechist might select a card that all will recite at the communal prayer time; or the children who can write may want to copy a particular card. Even for those children who can neither read nor write yet, the prayer cards accentuate the preciousness of the Word and help the children to realize that God's Word is written as well as spoken.

Conclusion

As we have said, all of Montessori pedagogy, if properly interpreted and applied, prepares within the child a fertile ground for prayer. Likewise, we can say that the life of the atrium springs from its being a place of prayer: a place of listening and responding to God, a place where work and study spontaneously become meditation, contemplation, and prayer.

In this shared religious experience, which we, as catechists, are called to live with the children, there is only one true Teacher, who is Christ himself. Although we have the important task of carefully preparing the environment, presenting the Christian Proclamation, and guiding the children in their use of the environment, our most important task is that of patiently observing the children and learning to listen to them and with them. Both our own joy to be living a religious experience with children, as well as our effectiveness as catechists, rests in our desire and commitment to listen to God with the children.

Appendixes

Gianna[1]

Sofia Cavalletti

Why is it so difficult for me to write about Gianna when we have spent almost half a century united by friendship and by work? When people ask me about her, when I take up my pen to write about her, I seem to remember nothing. And yet I feel her always so close to me, to the point that I overflow with joy when I see a person who might look like her in some way, and I continuously think, "I must tell this to Gianna," or "I have to show this to Gianna."

Sofia Cavalletti and Gianna Gobbi

In order to be able to speak about her, I must begin from afar, finishing, perhaps, where I should begin. My memory of Gianna cannot be separated from her beautiful country house. These words must not make you think of a luxurious villa. I would like to underline the words *beautiful* and *countryside*. Gianna's house was beautiful because it had kept all of its rustic character. The countryside made it so beautiful and special.

The fields did not only surround it, but they seemed to creep into it through the doors and through every window (maybe they also penetrated through the walls). Every breeze brought in with it the soul of

1. Reprinted from "Gianna," *The Catechesis of the Good Shepherd Commemorative Journal: Gianna Gobbi 1919-2002* (Chicago: Catechesis of the Good Shepherd Publications, 2019), 5–6.

the fields, autumn fields the plow was preparing for the seed, or spring or summer fields wrapped with so many colors. And yet around the house there was quite a large space covered with gravel where if a weed tried to push up, it was immediately plucked out by the inexorable hoe of Gianna's sister, Natalia, or by Gianna herself.

Gianna's house had kept, within itself, the different aspects of the fields: the festive aspect of the mature fields and, at the same time, the roughness that they present after being plowed. Once, when Gianna came back to Rome after a brief spring country sojourn, I asked her, "How was the countryside?" She answered, "A bride!"

Gianna's passion for the country was not a romantic one. It was akin to the spirit of the Latin poet Virgil as expressed, not in his pastoral poem, the *Eclogues*, but in the poem dedicated to work in the fields, the *Georgics*.

Even the hospitality in Gianna's house had a special character. I do not want you to misunderstand it if I say it was rustic. With this word I want to express sincere cordiality, true simplicity, and the capacity to offer up for enjoyment the different aspects of the seasons.

Here and there in the house, sunflowers gave back some of the sunshine they had drunk in the fields. During the vintage, the most beautiful clusters of grapes, together with some leaves, brought the beauty of the vine all the way to the center of the dining table, which was enriched with the luxury of its colors.

Gianna's hospitality has never made me feel like a guest. She allowed me to divide my time between the hours spent with her and a time of solitude, when books often remained closed, because the attraction of the spectacle of the fields was too strong and made it impossible to divert my eyes from it. How many hours did I spend looking, spellbound, at the plowed fields—so severe, so coarse, so stark, so naked and poor, and so full of hope.

What shall I say about the wonderful sunsets, in which it seemed that a great painter had used all the shades of his palette! These sunsets set the barn afire like a flaring torch; with its few, small, and blocked windows, the barn seemed not to realize the beauty of the transformation that the sunset was working on its bricks, offering this beauty with generosity to anyone who looked at it. At the same time, the house stood by quietly with its doors and windows thrown open.

When the day ended, two other shows awaited us. If it was a cool night, a great blazing fireplace *(focolare)* dominated the wider ground-floor room, as it did in all the peasants' houses. Or we would stroll under the stars while Gianna tried to recognize the constellations and to remember their names.

That countryside and that house had an important part in Gianna's life. She had reconquered the house little by little, rescuing it from the tenant farmers, to whom she gave land in exchange. To furnish the house, Gianna had set in motion all of her capacity for fantasy—the fantasy life for which I called her "Moritz." Moritz was a character in the *Corriere dei Piccoli*, a little journal for children I read when I was young; he was always undertaking extraordinary projects that, contrary to those of Gianna, always ended in disasters. Gianna was capable of transforming an old object full of dust, more or less shapeless, discovered someplace, into a little table, or a stool, or a shelf, or some other thing with which she could furnish the various rooms of her house. If she saw something in an old storeroom or market, that to me looked absolutely useless, immediately, the wheels of Moritz's brain would begin spinning and find an ingenious use for it. Gianna accomplished her projects with the ant's philosophy: little by little. Her drawers were full of drawings of things fermenting in her head.

The countryside was both Gianna's cross and her delight. Bureaucratic complications gave her frequent headaches, but the headaches were greatly outweighed by her joy in every rose that bloomed, the mushrooms we would look for in the morning under the poplar trees, and above all, by the summer harvest. On these occasions, all of Gianna's "peasant" soul emerged. Gianna was always a cricket who moved quickly from one place to the other, often disappearing unexpectedly out of sight of her companions, but when the farm machines arrived for the harvest, the rapidity of her movements multiplied! She could be standing beside you, but the next moment you would see her as a tiny, tiny speck on the far side of the field or climbing a tractor. At night, she came back covered with dust, but very happy at having taken to the farmers' cooperative what the fields had given after the winter's sleep.

This quickness of movement earned her another nickname, "Little Mouse." The irony is that Gianna was in a continuous state of open warfare with mice, which made her invent the most mouse-icidal traps. In spite of this fact, some courageous mice would dare to dart out before her eyes. These mice aroused Gianna, more than ever, to mouse-icidal rages.

I have spoken of Gianna's countryside, because Gianna lived in relation to it with a spirit that I would define as religious. It is not possible to separate the peasant Gianna from the researcher and Montessori educator. In her, the soul of the educator and the soul of the "peasant" were combined in perfect unity, and both constituted her person.

The seasonal rhythms of the countryside entered into Gianna and forged in her the discipline she brought to her work as an educator. The countryside rhythms impose a discipline because they cannot be rushed but require you to wait patiently; they do not allow you to pretend, for example, that a geranium flowers out of season. Gianna had learned very well how to wait. Her "peasant" patience was linked in an absolutely natural way with her Montessorian attitude, an attitude that wishes the educator to know and respect the time of each child's maturation. As Gianna watched the slow changes in nature, she also knew how to watch, without attempting to hasten, the slow normalization of the child and his or her manifestation as a child of God. Gianna's knowing how to wait was the expression of a deep respect—a religious respect—in front of the manifestations of the miracle of life, in all its forms.

For us, Gianna's beautiful house was also a place of work. There, usually under the shadow of one of the mulberry trees, we reviewed the entire second volume of *The Religious Potential of the Child* together. I called this place "my belvedere," because from there a wide view opened on the Marches countryside that is so serene, so mild, and so "caressed" by the hands of man. In that beautiful countryside, the colors faded until they reached the mountains. Sometimes, depending on the weather, we worked in that enjoyable place we called the hut *(capanna)*, where the peasant atmosphere was made more evident by the presence of some farm tools and the big and small baskets that hung from the eaves ready to receive the white and black figs and the peaches that came from the trees growing in the vineyard. Maybe the peaches didn't look very nice, but they compensated with a wonderful perfume and a genuine flavor, which we no longer know in the cities. In the hut, the horizon was not as broad as the one we could see from my belvedere under the tree, but a gentle breeze blew in. In that place, which I also sometimes called, with a certain irony, *il roseto* (the rose garden) *delle Marche*, the roses peered in at the little windows and, together with the roses that Gianna had set on the table, delighted our eyes and inspired the little touches that the book's second volume required.

Several of our strips have been laid out on Gianna's bed, in front of the three open windows of her room invaded by the sun. In the feast of light of that room, we examined them, we reviewed them, we discussed them, and we declared them ready . . . for the next revision.

If we get to talking about work, it is more difficult for me to talk about Gianna. Her presence, her collaboration, is so familiar, so taken for granted. Everything was so intertwined between us. As a former child of the atrium said at Gianna's funeral, "In my memory, it was Gianna's work to take the children by the hand and lead them to the Word of God, while Sofia brought the Word of God to the children." In every material that I look at, I see Gianna's pencils and pens, and also my saws. There is no material that was only her work or only mine. This intertwining, so evident and visible in the atrium, corresponds to an intertwining of feelings, of agreements, of passions, that our relation created between us. I will never be grateful enough to Gianna for this friendship, and to Adele Costa Gnocchi, who made us meet. From this description you can understand the void that Gianna's absence has left in my life; a part of me was taken away with her death. You can also understand that, at least for now, I cannot write longer.

June 7, 2002

The Rhythm of the Catechesis: Let Us Learn from the Fields[1]

Sofia Cavalletti and Gianna Gobbi

In our world, everything seems to be accelerating, and we feel swept away by the momentum, which obviously has many positive aspects; consider the many favorable possibilities that it offers for communications and relationships. However, there is a place that escapes this hurried pace, which seems to be a law unto itself: the countryside, with its vegetation.

If, in autumn, you gaze at the lumps of earth in an arid field, you could imagine them completely covered with wheat; but to have the wheat really exist before your eyes, you must wait until the mysterious and invisible work of winter passes, when you can observe the signs of spring and summer in the sky. Only then can we see the golden fields and have the wheat we need for our bread. Even a small plant on the windowsill can teach us the same lesson. I would love to see my plants full of flowers, but they tell me, "It's not the season." One must wait.

The rhythm of nature is not accelerated; the four seasons still fill the whole year.

Plants display a wisdom, which we must recognize, even in the human field and particularly in that of education. And when I say "education," I mean that work we must develop toward others and, in a particular way, toward ourselves.

When we start to examine our lives in perspective, we realize that some parts of who we are today have their roots far in the past. We can recognize the slow fermentation taking place in the successive steps of our lives, even when we reach very far back. Could we have rushed this patient work? No. And yet to us, the results seem to be a sudden miracle, in the same way that a wheat field seems to flame up in gold. But how much secret work came before these events!

1. Reprinted from *The Catechesis of the Good Shepherd Commemorative Journal: Gianna Gobbi 1919-2002* (Chicago: Catechesis of the Good Shepherd Publications, 2019), 42.

It seems to me that the greatest secrets of our world are hidden (or perhaps revealed?) in daily life, in those phenomena that, precisely because they are daily, risk disappearing from our attention. The parables of the mustard seed, the yeast, the seed that falls to the ground to bear much fruit, do they not point to the fundamental aspects of life, inviting us to fix our gaze on those apparently banal phenomena that are constantly in front of us? But to see them we must have time. A quick glance is not enough to see the mystery of Life being fulfilled in the mustard seed, as it passes from something that is less to something that is more.

In our work of catechesis, there are those who would like to accelerate this slow process, to shorten both the personal and material periods of preparation. In these cases the desire to transmit, as quickly as possible, what has been received over time is mistaken.

Of course, to shorten the time needed to prepare materials or to order extra copies of the materials from a vendor or artist would simplify the work of many. But would there be a real advantage for us and for the children with whom we work? Would we not impede in ourselves that slow, continuous work, which comes to us, leading us little by little to recognize that a mysterious "vegetation", is being completed in us, the results of which we only discover at a certain moment with the surprise and joy that is experienced in front of a gift?

In our meetings, the process of returning to the same subjects, and watching as they expand before us, draws us ever deeper, so that bit by bit we become capable of focusing ourselves upon their most essential point. We are placed before the simplicity of great things—that simplicity in front of which we feel lost and attracted at the same time—because we are made to place our hands on the reality that the "simple" cannot be confined. But in order for the "simple" to unfold its secrets to us, we must have time.

The time we spend with our saws, our embroidery needles, and our colored pencils, in order to complete a project (which doesn't always seem to come out perfect), is it not for us a time of tranquil meditation, containing a perfect balance between heart and mind? Of course, a professional could do it more beautifully but wouldn't we have lost the treasure? And if, as they often do, the children ask, "Who made this?" would we feel happier to answer, "Some manufacturer or some artist," or to be able to say, "These materials aren't perfect, but I made them with . . . "? Has a child ever said to you, "How ugly you made it"? It has never happened to us, even though I'm a mediocre carpenter and Gianna is not at the level of Leonardo.

Biography of Gianna Gobbi[1]

Ann Garrido

Gianna Gobbi was born in Rome on December 15, 1919, but a significant part of her youth—and adulthood—was spent on her family's farm in Senigallia, which she referred to as *la campagna* or "the country." This property near the Adriatic Sea only a short distance from Maria Montessori's childhood home in Chiaravalle raises the possibility the two women were distantly related. What is certain is that after learning about Montessori's work, Gobbi decided to enroll in a Montessori training course taught by Adele Costa Gnocchi at the Istituto Nazareth in Rome from 1939 to 1940.

Costa Gnocchi—an early collaborator of Montessori—became an important figure in Gobbi's life. In the years following her Montessori training, Gobbi worked in Costa Gnocchi's "little school" at Palazo Taverna in the center of Rome—a school that remained nameless in order to avoid drawing the attention of the Fascist government that had shuttered similar Montessori houses. Observing Gobbi's presence with children, Costa Gnocchi—who shared Montessori's interest in the intersection between Montessori methodology and faith formation—thought Gobbi would have particular gifts as a catechist.

In 1954, Costa Gnocchi introduced Gobbi to Sofia Cavalletti, a Scripture scholar and friend who had approached Costa Gnocchi about the best way of working with children preparing for the sacraments. Cavalletti would later write:

> I cannot think back without emotion to that first encounter with Gianna and the little group of children long ago. . . . We were thinking it would only be the first of a limited number of meetings before each of us returned to our field of work. Instead, it signaled the beginning of an impassioned and thrilling work with children that opened

1. Reprinted from *A Year with Sofia Cavalletti* (Chicago: Catechesis of the Good Shepherd Publications, 2017), 337–339.

> up for us always wider horizons in the world of childhood. (Foglietto no. 7, 2007)

Gobbi soon became Cavalletti's close collaborator. The two taught in several of the same schools—not only Costa Gnocchi's, but also the Armando Diaz Professional Institute and Virgil State High School, where during the 1960s and '70s Gobbi led home economics courses and Cavalletti taught religion within the Montessori departments of the schools. But their deepest collaboration took place at 34 Via degli Orsini. Engaging Montessori's earlier concept of the "atrium" as a starting point, the two developed a wide range of materials and presentations for children through an ongoing process of experimentation that lasted nearly fifty years. Originally participating families called the project the Montessori School of Religion, and the first move to organize and support the effort—coordinated by Costa Gnocchi in 1963—was named the Maria Montessori Association for the Religious Formation of the Child. But shortly thereafter it became more widely known as the Center of Catechesis of the Good Shepherd.

Gobbi and Cavalletti first published their joint insights in *Teaching Doctrine and Liturgy: The Montessori Approach* (available in Italian in 1961, English in 1964). As their thoughts developed with time, Cavalletti produced a significantly revised volume, *The Religious Potential of the Child* (available in Italian in 1978, English in 1983) followed by a second volume focused on older children (available in Italian in 1996, in English in 2002). Although these volumes were published under Cavalletti's name alone, she readily acknowledged Gianna's contribution to them:

> Of my many collaborators I will name only Gianna Gobbi. She is the one to represent the many others, my dearest friend among dearest friends, who, from our earliest beginnings in 1954, has brought to our common work her knowledge of the child . . . and her personal wisdom, the strength of her intuition and intelligence. (*Religious Potential, 6 to 12*, xiv)

While Gobbi continued to assist with Montessori courses locally, she also travelled with Sofia frequently for catechist formation courses—including trips to Mexico, Canada, the United States, and

Croatia. She later gathered her own lecture themes for publication in the book *Listening to God with Children* (available in Italian in 1992, in English in 1998). Gobbi coauthored *The Good Shepherd and the Child: A Joyful Journey* with Cavalletti and colleagues Silvana Montanaro and Patricia Coulter (available in English in 1994). And she assisted with the development of the *Io sono il Buon Pastor* workbooks and guidebooks designed for Italian school children and embraced widely in Latin America.

Gobbi worked alongside Cavalletti until her death on January 29, 2002, from complications following a fall. In her moving tribute to Gianna, Cavalletti wrote,

> In every material that I look at, I see Gianna's pencils and pens, and also my saws. There is no material that was only her work or only mine. This intertwining, so evident and visible in the atrium, corresponds to an intertwining of feelings, of agreements, of passions, that our relation created between us. I will never be grateful enough to Gianna for this friendship, and to Adele Costa Gnocchi, who made us meet. ("Gianna," in *Catechesis of the Good Shepherd: Essential Realities*, ed. Tina Lillig [Chicago: Liturgy Training Publications, 2004])